EVERYTHING I HOLD SACRED

EVERYTHING I HOLD SACRED

A Biography of the Spiritual Healer

Rev. Marian Butler

With

B. W. JONES

Regency Press (London & New York) Ltd.
125 High Holborn, London WC1V 6QA

*I dedicate this book to my Temple of Light Church
and to my friend and colleague Wayne Jones.*

ISBN 0 7212 0849 5

Printed and bound in Great Britain by
Buckland Press Ltd., Dover, Kent.

CONTENTS

LIST OF ILLUSTRATIONS

ACKNOWLEDGEMENTS

I would like to express my grateful thanks to Wayne Jones for helping me write this book, without his help this book would not have been written. I would also like to acknowledge the efforts of both Barry Howell and John Bowen for their helpful comments on the text. My thanks also to Lilwen Thomas and Lynnette Mason for typing some of the manuscript.

I will always be grateful to my late beloved Aunt Bess for letting me have the use of her humble home for my first Spiritual Healing Sanctuary. Without her love, help and support, when I was fighting for my own Spiritual existence, I doubt that I could have fought for what I believe in alone. Much of what I have been able to achieve in life is attributable to her.

Above all, I thank God for the precious gift that He bestowed upon me.

REV. MARIAN BUTLER.

FOREWORD
by Ray Branch

Some years ago at a Seminar held at the Harry Edwards Spiritual Healing Sanctuary for both advanced and aspiring spiritual healers, I said: "I do not know of any Healer – Harry Edwards included – who has not at some time or another in his or her life, gone through some personal hellfire or suffering. In fact I would go on to say that 'The steel of the healer is forged in the fires of suffering.' These latter words could hardly apply more aptly than to Marian Butler or, to give her her proper title, The Reverend Marian Butler, who has been a leading figure in the world of Spiritual Healing for over forty years.

Her triumph over physical illness and adversity as a child is a story in itself, but here we have the full picture of a woman who very early on in life recognised the great gifts bestowed upon her, not only that of healing but of those other much-treasured gifts of the Spirit, clairaudience and clairvoyance; and having combined them all with her unshakeable Christian beliefs, she can now look back on a life of true service and fulfilment, in the knowledge that her splendid healing gift in particular has taken her all over the world, where she has lectured on the subject, counselled and guided so many in the science and application of healing, and in her capacity as a Minister has truly preached the Gospel of Christ in all her work.

Throughout her life Marian Butler has claimed nothing for herself as far as healing triumphs are concerned, fully recognising that she has simply been an open channel for the spirit of love and compassion to flow through in abundance for the benefit of those who are sick. She pays ample tribute to her hosts of spirit mentors and was a great friend of the greatest spiritual healer of modern times, Harry Edwards, who held her in high esteem, not only for her healing work, but for her warm and buoyant character, for Marian is one of those people whose sparkling personality lights up any occasion.

One of the highlights of her story is in her own explanation of what spiritual healing is all about, and is in itself an excellent and concise treatise on the subject, with fascinating case-histories from her healing work.

Marian, always an ardent and fearless campaigner, makes a strong plea for spiritual healing and medical science to combine for the benefit of all mankind, echoing the very sentiments of Harry Edwards. Her account of a vision and conversation she held with him long ago after his passing, upon one of her visits to Israel when she went to Emmaus, just outside Jerusalem, is just another example of her close affinity with the world of Spirit and, indeed, a world that she brings vividly to life as she recounts an address given through her mediumship to an audience in her own splendid church, so aptly named "The Temple of Light". For if ever there is a monument to achievement built from nothing by a dedicated woman who had nothing but a blazing Christian faith and belief, then her church will stand for all time, not only as a place of worship and healing for the sick, but as a monument of triumph over opposition, scorn, and human spite which would have broken a lesser person; but her "Temple of Light" will be forever synonymous with the name of Marian Butler, whose life and healing work has truly brought light into the hearts and minds of thousands throughout her glittering career.

RAY BRANCH,
The Harry Edwards
Spiritual Healing Sanctuary,
Burrows Lea,
Shere,
Guilford,
Surrey.

9

INTRODUCTION

The Rev. Marian Butler is a Past President of the World Federation of Healing, former Chairperson of the Welsh Healers' Association, and Founder of the Temple of Light Spiritual Healing Sanctuary at Ystradgynlais, near Swansea, South Wales, and has been a distinguished Spiritual Healer for the past forty-five years.

The Rev. Butler was a great friend of the late Harry Edwards, by whom she was held in the highest esteem. She also trained with and learned a great deal from Harry Edwards, who she affectionately called, "The Rolls Royce of all Healers". Always known for her honest forthright views, she is one never to exaggerate, indulge in personal ego trips or flights of fancy.

As a very young child she found that she could 'see' and 'hear' images and voices that other people could not. During her childhood and also later in life, she suffered from many serious illnesses which sometimes threatened her life. She has known most forms of physical and emotional pain and has suffered deprivation, degredation, humiliation and sometimes even hatred. These experiences helped make her even more determined to fight for her beliefs. Like most mediums, she feels that such trials were specific acts of Spirit, which were necessary in order that she could develop the qualities of deep awareness, compassion and love, which are prerequisites for a healing to take place.

After her mother died, her Aunt Bess who lived next door looked after her as if she was her own daughter. In 1951, Aunt Bess gave the largest room of her small terraced home to Marian, for use as a Spiritual Healing Sanctuary. During almost four decades, approximately one hundred and forty to one hundred and sixty patients per week came to her for healing. In that period alone, about 250,000 patients passed through her healing hands. After decades of work for Spirit in her little home, she saved all the monies that had been raised through donations and fund-raising, so that at the age of seventy-one years she eventually accumulated enough money to raise a deposit for her own church.

This was purpose-built, with Healing and Meditation rooms, and was opened in 1987. As prophesied by Spirit, the debt of the church was cleared within four years of its opening.

During her eventful life she has taught and lectured about healing and mediumship throughout the U.K. and in countries such as Austria, Australia, Canada, New Zealand, Germany, Denmark, Holland, Israel, Switzerland, and across much of the United States of America.

At the age of seventy-four years she had formed and trained her own team of Spiritual Healers and counsellors to work for Spirit. As she says: "I will work all my life for Spirit, I want to die with my boots on."

Chapter One

THE EARLY DAYS

From the day that I was born I was very blessed to have two wonderful women in my life. My mother was taken seriously ill with Empyema of the lungs just two days after giving birth to me. I cannot recall all the details, but I did not see her again until I was about three years of age. She had to have one lung and four ribs removed. My Aunt Elizabeth Ann Thomas who lived next door to us, lost her only child from meningitis. Since my mother was ill, my aunt looked after me as if I was her own daughter.

My brothers David Ewart and William Rees Butler, continued to live with my father, David John Butler. He was a good man who we all revered. After surgery, my mother spent a few years in a convalescent home. When she eventually returned home, she naturally wanted me to live with her again. My aunt became very distressed, since I had become like a daughter to her. She was often found crying and full of sadness. My mother comforted her by saying, "You will not lose her completely, after all, we only live next door." In her kindness, my mother arranged that I spent half my time eating meals in her house and the other half with my aunt. This situation resulted in me having two very good mothers. Just before my mother passed away, I was about twenty-six years old, I lived permanently with my aunt. Aunt Bess, as we affectionately called her, effectively took on the role of my mother and confidante. Aunt Bess was very kind and loving to me during mother's long periods of sickness. When I became involved with Spiritual Healing, she was always supportive and would reassure me by saying, that if the work that I was doing was right and true, then I should carry on.

I was the first person in our family to be blessed with the psychic gift. Aunt Bess was always a pillar of strength to me and always supported me when my own spirit was low. To me she was my mother, father, sister, brother, comforter and helper and my source of strength all rolled into one. Although she passed away on the 19th May, 1974, at the age of eighty-two, I cannot say that she has ever left me. I always feel her near me, every day of my life. Consequently I never fear the Spirit World. I am only fearful when the Spirit World is not around.

My aunt was what I affectionately called 'a true warrior', she would fight for what was right and true. She was always fighting the losing battles of others. Her spirit of justice was very strong. She was what the Welsh people would call a true 'character'. She would give her last penny to anyone who was in need of it, and would, so to speak, take the shirt off her back to help anyone. She was not a wealthy person by any means, but never saw want. Equally, no one saw want when Auntie was around. She also had the ability to find missing persons. How she did this I do not know, I never discussed it with her. Often I would accidentally hear her on the telephone counselling some person who was distressed. She never considered herself to be a healer. I, however, considered her to be a healer of the soul, because she always gave to people what they were searching for. She was a wonderful singer and could have become a wonderful actress. Her other sister, my Aunt Gwen, received professional voice-training. Aunt Bess, however, did not receive such a privilege. Whenever there was housework or the washing up to be done, Aunt Bess would naturally ask her sister Gwen to help her. Invariably Gwen would reply by saying that she had to practise on the piano. Gwen had a beautiful, trained voice, but her voice was not as good as Aunt Bess's, for Aunt Bess had a natural love for music.

In those days, the local chapels would hold singing competitions, and invariably both Aunt Gwen and Aunt Bess would compete. Aunt Gwen never got a chance of winning if Aunt Bess was also singing. The first prize would be a heart-shaped, velvet handbag, with a ribbon on it so that it could be hung around the neck. The handbag also contained a handsome prize of sixpence (two and a half pence today). Aunt Bess accumulated many handbags, and she would offer to share them with her sister Gwen. Gwen would reply, "I don't want the handbag or the sixpence. I just want to win."

"Come and wash the dishes then, then I will not compete."

During the Second World War, like many other people, she took in evacuees. She was friendly with the local Scout Master who was known as Mr. "Skip" Morgan who later obtained an M.B.E. for his work in the Scouting movement. "Skip" Morgan was a teacher who was highly regarded by everyone in the locality. Although he did not visit us all that often, he was always a welcome sight. We all had a tremendous respect for him and his work with Scouts. Incidentally, his brother (Llew) was a very good photographer. He was also a spiritualist, who had an interest in psychic photography. Because of her friendship with "Skip", Auntie encouraged all the evacuees to join the Scouts. All the evacuees loved her because she looked after them as if they were her own children. In total Auntie received four groups of evacuees. Our house was more like an orphanage!

On one occasion, the evacuees staying with Aunt Bess had been given a list of food items to take to camp by Mr. "Skip" Morgan. During the war days, most of the food was rationed and people who cared for evacuees would get a money allowance. One of the items on the camp list was custard powder. When she came to claim her allowance from the local council, she found that payment had been stopped. Auntie was naturally enraged by this outrage and marched down to see the local Clerk of the Council and demanded the money that he had "stolen" from her.

"I have not stolen any money of yours," said the Clerk.

"Oh yes you have, you have stolen my children's allowance for the evacuees," replied Auntie. "Here is a list that "Skip" Morgan gave the boys to take to camp and here are the receipts of payment."

"You can't claim for custard powder these days," said the Clerk.

"Custard powder, don't you like dessert too?" said Auntie.

"I want every penny that you owe me and I won't leave here until I get it."

Needless to say, Auntie got her reimbursement. Justice once again had been done. Sometime later, Auntie once again found herself in conflict with the Clerk of the Council over the evacuees. On this occasion the evacuees were accompanied by their mothers, who were also sisters. One mother and her two children stayed with my mother next door, whilst the other sister and her two children stayed with Auntie. Despite all her efforts she could not exercise her control over the children. In particular she was very annoyed with them for not washing their clothes. This caused her house to smell, which in turn annoyed Auntie even more. Finally she gave the children an ultimatum! They should either wash their clothes or she would put them out in the street. She informed the Clerk of the Council, who in turn informed her that since it was a weekend, he could not take any action until Monday.

"No!" Auntie replied most emphatically. "The same law that will put them out on Monday will apply today. They must wash their clothes."

When the children left that day, she gave them some extra food and clothing that she had made especially for them. Auntie got her justice and administered it fairly.

Auntie always took extreme pride in the fact that she did not owe anybody anything. She was a true giver in its deepest sense and was never a taker. When she died in May, 1974, I will always remember the words of the minister who buried her:

' . . . and now to nature's great storehouse we consign the garment borrowed from it."

Without Auntie's love and support I doubt that I could have fought for what I believe in alone. Much of what I have been able to achieve in life is a tribute to her love, honesty, tenacity and freedom of spirit.

Marian Butler at about ten years of age.
Notice the deformed left leg following Rheumatic Fever.

Ann Elizabeth Thomas – "Aunt Bess".

Chapter Two

FIRST EXPERIENCES

As a young child, even before I started school, I was always unwell. I suffered from anaemia and very painful rheumatic joints. Although I cannot remember the exact details, I can clearly remember feeling almost continuously weak and unwell. My joints would hurt and were very painful if I moved them, which of course, prevented me from playing with other little children in the neighbourhood. Through all this suffering, I can also clearly remember that my mother was always loving and caring. Although academically, she was not a scholar, I always considered her to be a very wise and learned person. She too had suffered various forms of illness, which in turn must have made her very mindful of my own suffering.

When I was about six years of age, I felt my health improve a little. This slight improvement, however, was short-lived. I can quite vividly remember the development of pains in my back. I cannot remember how long these pains lasted, but it took me a very long time before I was free of such pain. I later learned from my mother that I had developed pleurisy. These events caused me to lose many months of schooling. Sometime later, I cannot remember exactly how long, I developed a rash all over my body. The doctors who treated me did not know what type of rash it was, but thought that it was nettle-rash. This illness was very upsetting to me, the whole area of my skin was subject to constant irritation, which often drove me frantic. Mother's constant care, together with her insistence that I ate various vitamin supplements, eventually resulted in an improvement in my health state. Her constant love and attention, together with the application of a zinc ointment supplied by the doctor, resulted in my recovery.

Unfortunately, this brief respite was short-lived. Not long after my recovery from my skin complaint, I began to suffer from continual violent headaches and sore throats. The doctor attributed this latest condition to the fact that my blood was in a very poor condition, despite all the food and various supplements that my mother had given me. I sometimes suffer from similar headaches today, especially when I look at the colour of purple. If I look at this colour for longer than about a minute or so, I begin to find the pressure building up in my head, which will eventually cause a violent headache. Many people, including mediums, have suggested various ways of counteracting these headaches, unfortunately none of these suggestions has formed a solution to my problem. I have never fully discovered why the purple colour should affect me in such a way. I assume it is because of my involvement in psychic matters over so many years. As the reader may realise, purple is generally considered to be a spiritual colour; i.e. one of the highest vibrational frequencies in the visual colour spectrum. I assume that in some way my own spirituality, perhaps unconsciously, resonates or interferes with the purple colour, which in turn causes my violent headaches. The only cure to the problem that I have found is to avoid looking at purple or violet colours in the first place, even if they are to be found in the form of beautiful pansies or violets.

I cannot say that as a young child I enjoyed life as a normal young girl would have done. I was not able to play like other young children, because I was mostly confined to my bed. At one time polyneuritis was surging through my whole being. I also suffered from an ulcerated stomach, consequently, I knew what it was like to suffer tremendous pain. However, this pain was nothing to compare with the pain that I endured when I sustained an accident at the age of seven. It was in March, 1922, when a slate fell off the roof of the Ynyscedwyn primary school at which I was a pupil, as a consequence of a gale force wind. As it fell, it collided with a lean-to building at the side of the school. A piece of slate landed on the top of my head, knocking me unconscious and causing profuse bleeding.

I was given some first aid treatment by the headmaster and his teaching staff. The local doctor, a Doctor Walsh, was called to examine me and I was taken home to rest. A few weeks later, I developed severe headaches, and as a result, the doctor came to visit me again. He diagnosed, to his amazement, that the cut at the top of my head had caused septicaemia.

In the days that followed, my head had swollen to an enormous size. The doctor came to see me three times a day to lance the head wound. Later, this decreased to twice-daily visits. This routine continued for several weeks until a piece of slate came away from the wound, and after this, my head started to heal. Eventually it was discovered that I had suffered a fractured skull and encephalitis, an inflammatory condition of the brain. Slowly I began to recover and I improved to such an extent that I was allowed to start school again, but for afternoon sessions only. I was still very weak at this time. One day, I noticed that I had begun to lose the sight in my eyes and by the end of that week I had become totally blind. I could not distinguish night from day, but thank God, my sight returned one week later, however, I had truly experienced blindness. As a young girl of about eleven years, I suffered from shingles, which occurred around my waist. This was also a very unpleasant experience. In latter years, when I was about sixty-two years of age, I encountered this painful condition again. This time however, the shingles occurred in my head which in turn permanently affected the sight in my right eye.

As I approached puberty, I felt that I was at last beginning to reach a better state of health, yet paradoxically I was suffering tremendous pain in my upper arms and neck. That pain remains vivid in my mind even until today. If someone is suffering from pains in the shoulder or neck area, I have the deepest sympathy for them. Such pains can leave the arms feeling very heavy, at the same time, the pain can make one feel very depressed.

So during the whole of my childhood, until I became a teenager, I can honestly say that hardly a month went by without me suffering from one form of illness or another. In my own mind, I am sure that all these illnesses were due to some kind of blood deficiency. My mother had suffered from Empyema of the lungs. She was so badly infected that she had to have one of her lungs removed, not long before I was born. Because mother's lungs were so poor, her blood may have been deficient in oxygen, which in turn, may have affected the quality of my own blood. I was very close to my mother and loved her very dearly and I never blamed her for my poor health. Today, I am convinced that all that physical suffering was to be my training, so that I could understand the different forms of physical suffering in this world. However, as I approached my mid teens I eventually threw off the cloak of sickness which always seemed to be about me. This welcome change in my health state left me feeling full of life and vigour, my body seemed to have been recharged and at last I was fully active and full of strength. This was a source of tremendous joy to me. At last I could run or walk just like other teenagers, without pain. I had my first taste of good health, which most people around me had taken for granted.

Before the Second World War, I came into contact with Mr. James Griffiths, who later became a Member of Parliament for Burry Port. He was a native of Ystradgynlais. His wife and my mother were close friends. Mr. Griffiths and I had many long conversations together, for in some way, he seemed to be taking an interest in my work. During our meetings I informed him that he would become a member of the Government. I also told him that his work would in some way be involved with insurance. He later became the Minister responsible for Social Security in the Labour Government of 1947!

Later, I met a gentleman who lived in Neath Abbey. He and his wife had become disturbed and very anxious about a missing person in their family. Mr. James Griffiths brought these people to see me. I can remember insisting to see the husband and wife separately, since I felt that seeing them at the same time would cause some kind of confusion in my mind. I was only a teenager at this time. As I spoke to the husband, I had the firm impression of a book being opened, only to find empty pages, with no writing on them. I recalled to him what I had seen and repeated that the book was empty.

"Does this mean that he has passed on?" asked the husband.

"I don't know what it means," I replied.

I conversed with him for about thirty minutes, trying to reassure him, but the whole time the words "Empty Pages" kept recurring in my mind. When he left, I sat down with his wife, and as she sat down, I had the impression that we were both entering an empty room, absent of all furnishings. The room was completely empty but for an electric light bulb. I could not explain the meaning of this to her and I could see from the look on her face that she was very disappointed. Later, when Mr. James Griffiths came to see me again, he informed me that they were due to go on holiday and asked on their behalf if they could come and see me again when they returned. Unfortunately, I never saw that couple again, since three weeks later they both died. This explained to me the "Empty Pages" and the "Empty Room" that I had previously visualised.

I now realised that after a long period of suffering, my psychic faculty had begun to develop. According to my parents, David and Margaret Butler, it had begun to develop from about three years of age. At that time they were living in 8 Glanley Street, Ystradgynlais. (Today the same house has the address of 26 Heol Maes-y-Dre). I had already begun 'seeing' and 'hearing' but I have no recollection of these events, I can remember 'hearing' voices at five years of age. I was able to relate to events years before I was born, and certain aspects of what had happened to people and their families, aspects which I could not possibly have known about.

During the period when I was suffering from the effects of the accident to my head, Dr. Walsh would say to my mother:

"Mrs. Butler, has she been seeing and hearing some funny things today?"

"Oh yes she has," my mother would reply.

"Oh don't take any notice, it is her sickness you know, imagination plays a very important part with children," said the doctor.

This conversation carried on almost every time Dr. Walsh visited me, always asking my mother the same question. In turn the doctor always came up with the same reply:

"It is her sickness you know!"

During one of these occasions, as he left my bedroom to go down the staircase and into the hallway, a young boy appeared before me and said to me in an Irish accent.

"You don't have to listen to him, he is my father you know!"

"What happened to you?" I asked.

"I died," he said. "I was riding my bike and I broke my head against a wall." Later, I discovered that he had fractured his skull.

I kept this conversation with the Irish boy close to my heart. When the doctor called again the next day, he asked my mother the same old question: "Has she been seeing or hearing some funny things again today?"

"Yes," said my mother.

"Oh take no notice," said Dr. Walsh in his usual manner.

"That's not what Arthur says," I said, from my bed.

"Arthur, your son, says he was riding his bike and broke his head against a wall."

"Oh my God!" exclaimed the doctor.

"Can you tell me where I was living in Ireland?" asked Dr. Walsh.

"I don't know, but I can ask Arthur," I said.

"Surely he has not forgotten where we lived," Arthur said to me. "It was in Cork."

This incident proved that I was not imagining these things, consequently, my parents began to take notice of me. My faculty continued to grow. Then one day, my parents decided to give me a severe dressing-down, telling me of the dangers and the pitfalls that I was letting myself in for. I was informed that if I continued with this course of life that I had entered into, I would be prosecuted and certified as insane. This never materialised and my psychic faculty continued to grow.

At the age of about fourteen, I shook off the cloak of sickness. I started to live again, taking part in all the activities that young teenage girls do, I even joined a youth club. I went from job to job for I never seemed to be satisfied with my situation. I was like a rolling stone. I cannot fully explain how I felt, it was not as if I was unhappy in my work or that I could not get on with my colleagues, but there seemed to be something driving me to experience and to learn from life as much as I could. It was as if I wanted to compensate for my early sickness and lack of education.

My first job was in domestic service at Eaton Crescent, Swansea, working for a Mrs. Walters. She was a very demanding woman, her whole attitude was one of superiority, with us servants being of a very low status in life. It was a very large house with a very demanding work schedule. I would start work at 5.50 a.m. and would not finish until after 11.00 p.m. Mrs. Walters had a son who I had to address as Master Jack. As time progressed I sensed that part of me was rebelling against her injustice.

She was very strict and would only allow half a day off each week together with every Sunday so that I could go home and visit my mother. However, I always had to be back indoors before 10.00 p.m. One afternoon I decided that I would go and visit mother in Ystradgynlais. On the return journey the bus broke down in the village of Clydach, which resulted in me arriving back at Mrs. Walter's residence after the 10.00 p.m. deadline. For this misdemeanour I was severely reprimanded and ordered to bed. I felt that this treatment was but another injustice which was beyond all reason. After all, I had not done anything wrong.

Sometime later, mother came to Swansea to do some shopping, and naturally she invited me to join her. On hearing of this, Mrs. Walters invited mother to have tea with her. I could not understand this since the invite was totally out of character with her autocratic nature. A week prior to mother's visit, an event happened which first sowed the seeds for my eventual departure. It occurred when a woman knocked on Mrs. Walter's door and I went to answer, and being a young girl of only fourteen years of age, I was not accustomed with formal etiquette. The woman asked me if Mrs. Walters was at home.

"Yes," I replied and I asked her to wait at the door as I went to the drawing-room to fetch Mrs. Walters.

I informed Mrs. Walters, "There is a woman at the door Ma'am, who wishes to speak to you."

Mrs. Walters followed me to the front door, and I returned to the kitchen. I was in the kitchen for about five minutes when Mrs. Walters sent for me and made me re-enact the scene of the woman's arrival at the door. Mrs. Walters said to me, "You told me there was a woman at the door, what you should have said is: 'there is a lady at the door.' You should also have addressed the lady as her Ladyship."

Mrs. Walters asked the lady to go outside, and told me to address her properly this time. Naturally this annoyed me very much, since it seemed to me that the whole charade was merely a grotesque aspect of snobbery.

When mother arrived the following week to have tea with Mrs. Walters, she soon realised that I was fully earning my wages, which in total only amounted to nine shillings (forty-five pence today) per week.

On meeting mother, Mrs. Walters said to her that she had raised a very good daughter, who was clean, hardworking and honest. "However, she has only one fault", she added, "she always tends to speak her own mind."

After tea she asked mother to leave all the crockery on the table. "I will clear up," said Mrs. Walters. At the time I thought this was exceptionally kind of her. Mother and I went to the cinema and I was allowed to be back by 10.10 p.m., the extra ten minutes allowed me just sufficient time for me to see mother safely on her bus. When I arrived back at Eaton Crescent, I immediately noticed that the tea dishes still remained on the table. When I entered the sitting-room Mrs. Walters said, "You must wash the dishes before you go to bed, and by the way, your mother is a very nice woman." Remembering the experience with her ladyship the previous week my rebellious nature forced me to reply, "Excuse me Ma'am, my mother is a lady!" From that moment on our relationship deteriorated and Mrs. Walters became even more hostile towards me.

In retrospect, that was probably the first experience in my life that made me stand up for myself and to become a 'warrior' and fight against the injustices of life. A few days later Mrs. Walters organised a bridge party for twelve guests. She used this occasion to punish my rebellious nature by making me work overtime to ensure that all preparations for the party were complete.

At this time, my Uncle Richard Butler was a minister of religion in Swansea and also worked in the Seamen's Union. One Sunday, my uncle invited me to have lunch with him and his wife. As I was preparing for my visit, and even though it was my day off, Mrs. Walters threw one of her regular tantrums and stopped me from going out and found extra duties for me to do. The following day uncle called around to find out why I had not accepted his invitation. When he arrived at the front door he was met by Mrs. Walters. After explaining who he was, he was told to go to the back door and meet me in the servants' quarters. This made me realise that even the church was subservient to her bigotry and spitefulness. During the visit uncle informed me that he did not like the idea of me working there. He told me that the days of slavery had long passed. In his kindness, he offered me the opportunity of moving into his home whenever I wanted.

On the following Saturday Mrs. Walters informed me, "By the way Marian, you can cancel your arrangements for tomorrow, you are not to go out of this house, I have extra duties for you." On Sunday I spent a very miserable day working until 1.00 a.m. on Monday morning. Despite having worked until this late hour, I was instructed to be up again at 4.30 a.m. so that Mr. Walters could have an early breakfast before setting out on a business trip. In the very early hours of that Monday morning it suddenly dawned on me that I did not have to put up with this situation any longer. Although I was tired, I did not go to sleep, I packed my case before 4.30 a.m. When I got up I made myself the first full breakfast that I had eaten in months. In all the time that I had worked there, I had never had a meal of my own, I always had to eat the unwanted leftovers from Mrs. Walters' meals. At about 5.30 a.m. I walked out of Eaton Crescent and never set foot on the premises again. At the gate I was met by the postman who said to me, "I wondered how long you would last, for she cannot keep a maid for more than two months." On hearing his words I smiled to myself, for I had lasted almost twelve months!

After leaving I went straight to see Uncle Richard, and on the following day my aunt took me to an employment agency in Swansea, where I was offered a job at Leavesdon Private Nursing Home, Ambleside Drive, in Oxford, which was run by a Mrs. Clark. I was accepted for a trial period only on the basis of a reference given by Uncle Richard. The nursing home dealt with all kinds of illnesses for both children and adults. Mrs. Clark was always very kind to me and explained that there was no need for me to do any physical work.

My main duties were to deliver food-trays to the patients at meal-times. I was also instructed to read to the patients and run any errands for them. My remaining duties involved washing dishes after meal-times. Although I had a liberal amount of time off, I hardly went outside of the grounds of the nursing home, since most of my wages were spent on replacing all the fine crockery that I broke during washing-up! All the chinaware was beautiful and delicate, matching the individual decor of each room.

Unfortunately the chinaware was far too delicate for me to handle! It was almost a month before I accumulated enough money to go outside the grounds. This was only achieved by Mrs. Clark giving me a sub from my wages. She was always very kind and helpful to me. She even taught me how to smoke cigarettes!

Even though everyone was very kind to me and the food and accommodation was excellent, I never knew what it was like to get a good night's sleep. This was because my beautiful living-quarters were next to the labour room where babies seemed to be born continuously every hour. However, after about three weeks I was so tired that neither the screams of the mothers nor the babies could awaken me. In total, I worked in the nursing home for about nine months. This period in my life was to be my first contact with sick people.

I used to enjoy walking along the streets to Magdalen College. My presence among the Colleges of Oxford seemed to stimulate my mind, and the fact that so many learned people had studied there made me feel that it was a great privilege to be there.

In hindsight, my new job in Oxford was the beginning of my Spiritual unfoldment. Often on my way back to the nursing home I had to pass a very beautiful old tree. Even though I could fully appreciate its majesty, I was always very frightened every time I walked past it. Why, I did not know. It always left me with the sensation that eyes were watching me, I always tried to go home before it was dark and I would run past the tree as fast as my legs would carry me. One day I mentioned these feelings to Matron Clark, who turned to me and said, "It is funny that you should say that Marian, are you psychic or something?" She continued by explaining that a man had committed suicide by hanging himself from that tree. A few weeks later I was informed that mother had had a serious heart attack and it was with great sadness that I left Oxford.

On returning home, I lived with mother for about two to three years. As soon as she recovered, I began to get itchy feet again. I was still being driven to explore life. When I was about nineteen years of age I took up a job in a summer season boarding-house in a Jewish home of Mrs. Slater in Littlehampton near Bognor Regis. On my journey there I was accompanied by the member of Parliament, the Rt. Hon. James Griffiths, who wanted to make sure that I was met by reputable people. To his surprise we were met by Mrs. Slater's son, John Slater, who at that time was quite a famous actor. I had a very happy time in Littlehampton and my wages were quite good – amounting to eighteen shillings per week (ninety pence today). In addition, I received free accommodation and plentiful tips. I also had about four hours off every afternoon which enabled me to visit the cinema or see a show. After about nine months I sadly had to return home to be with mother who had become ill again.

I looked after mother for about three years and after she recovered I worked for a short period in a grocery store in Seven Sisters Road, Holloway, London, which was not far from Holloway Prison. Living so near to the prison I felt an urge to work in the prison service, but sadly this opportunity never did materialise.

After leaving Holloway I went to work as a chambermaid in the aristocratic area of St. James's Court, Westminster, London. I looked after three private flats. One belonged to a rich peer whose father was a shipping magnet. The second flat belonged to a retired colonel and his wife, Lady Mostyn, whose main residence was in North Wales. At one period all three flats became vacant for about a month since all the owners were away on holiday. This meant that I had virtually no work to do and found it very difficult to overcome the boredom.

One day I was tidying up her Ladyship's wardrobe when I noticed her new ball gown, tiara, fox cape, and beautiful new shoes. Her Ladyship and I were the same size, both being tall and slim. I could no longer resist the temptation to try her beautiful clothes on. I had just completed dressing when the door to the flat opened and I heard a voice bellowing ". . . and where do you think you are going?" For once in my life I was speechless.

"I would take those clothes off if I were you," said his Lordship. "Get back into your uniform and come and see me in my office at once."

After entering his office, he told me that he would terminate my employment immediately. By this time I had regained my speech and my faculties.

"I think that is rather unfair Sir," I replied.

"You had no business to wear her Ladyship's clothes," he retorted.

"Just as you had no business in breaking your marriage vows Sir." I bluntly replied.

I continued by reminding him of the mistresses that he had entertained in the flat.

"What would her Ladyship have to say about that?" I enquired. "I did not report you, so why should you sack me?"

By this time I was fully on the offensive and for a moment my employer was speechless. But he replied by saying, "You would not do that Marian!"

"You sack me, and I will spill the beans on you," I said. "If need be I will even go to the press."

On hearing this, the blood drained from his face and stuttering he replied, "Ah! I think it is your day off today, Marian is it not?"

"Yes Sir," I replied.

"Here is a pound note, go and buy yourself something. Be here again tomorrow as usual, but never, never, wear her Ladyship's clothes again. Now how is your lip?"

"Buttoned up Sir," I replied. And I kept my job for a further three years.

It was during my stay in St. James's Court that I first became involved in politics. I was in my early twenties and by this time I realised that although my psychic faculty had never deserted me, it began to reawaken again. However, at this time I never realised that I had the Healing gift.

As I was walking through London one day I heard my name being called by a gentleman, an old friend with a familiar Welsh accent.

"What on earth are you doing here Marian?" he enquired.

"I am working in St. James's Court," I replied.

"Where are you going now?" he asked.

"To the cinema in the Elephant and Castle," I replied.

"Oh no you are not, you are coming to the House of Commons with me."

It was around this period, when Neville Chamberlain was Prime Minister, that there was a hint of preparation for the Second World War.

Sometime later James Griffiths said to me, "I think the time has now come Marian to make you a regular visitor of the House of Commons." To my astonishment he supplied me with a permanent pass to enter the public gallery. On average, I used my pass two or three times per week and I found those visits to be one of the most stimulating, interesting and entertaining parts of my life. Often I would present my pass to the Sergeant at Arms in Westminster Hall, who would proclaim:

"James Griffiths, Member of Parliament for Burry Port . . . Marian Butler please step forward."

"This announcement would permit me to meet James Griffiths who would always greet me in the Welsh language . . . "Sut wyt ti?" . . . "How are you?"

Entry into the Houses of Parliament was a whole new experience to me and allowed me to meet many prominent politicians of the day. It also exposed me to the operation of power at the highest level. During this period, I had the opportunity of meeting many famous people such as Lord Boothby, Richard Crossman, Jim Maxton, Lady Astor and many others. I had tea with the German actor Conrad Veidt, and in the private bars in the House of Commons, I also had many private discussions on the balcony with Lloyd George and Aneurin Bevan. I learned a great deal from Aneurin Bevin.

One day he said to me, "Always stick to your guns Marian. Although I am not a religious man, like you I believe in justice."

When Aneurin Bevan died he had no religious ceremony, his ashes were simply spread upon the mountains overlooking his beloved homeland in Ebbw Vale, South Wales. Although he did not believe in my psychic work he often asked me questions about it and seemed to show a genuine interest. I will never forget his words to me: "If you believe in your God, you have as much right as anyone else in this world to believe in him."

On one visit to the House of Commons I can clearly remember Winston Churchill and Aneurin Bevan in the midst of a ferocious political debate. On this occasion, four policemen were summoned to remove them, but what astonished me most of all was that as they left the House, they were arm in arm, later to be found in the Commons bar having a drink together. Of course I should not have been so surprised, as Churchill and Aneurin Bevan were very close friends.

When mother came to visit me in London, she was ever so proud to accompany me to the House of Commons and hear of the many famous people that I had met. During my stay in St. James's I visited the House of Commons on more than two hundred occasions. I almost felt as if I was a permanent member there. It may be as a result of my closeness to the workings of Parliament, that many years later in November, 1964, whilst I was sitting with my spiritual friends, I had a clear vision of being inside the House of Commons. I also had the clear impression that the Speaker of the House was going to have an accident. The vision was so clear that I was compelled to write to the Prime Minister of what I had visualised. Some days later I read in the press that the Speaker of the House of Commons had had an accident whilst walking along the streets of London. Later I received a letter from the Prime Minister's Secretary thanking me for the letter that I had sent him.

Later that month I had another clear impression that Lord Boothby would be taken ill. A few days later I received a reply from Lord Boothby's Private Secretary informing me that Lord Boothby, on medical advice, had just departed for the West Indies for a long rest.

By 1939, the Second World War had been declared and my period at St. James's Court came to an end and I had taken up a new position as a production worker at a radio factory. Later, the factory was taken over to do work for the war effort. These events left me out of work, and for a short period of time I returned home. It was not long before I became bored and returned again to London to look for work.

I will never forget the London blitz period which millions had to endure. On many occasions, I can clearly remember having to go to the Underground air-raid shelter in Shepherds Bush. On one particular occasion I remember coming home from work and saying to my landlady, Mrs. Williams, "I am not going to the air-raid shelter in Shepherds Bush tonight, I am going to find the deepest underground shelter in London. I will be going to the underground shelter in Notting Hill!"

"Why go all that way? enquired Mrs. Williams. "We must stick together."

"I am definitely not going to Shepherds Bush tonight, I am going to the deepest shelter that I can find," I replied.

Reluctantly, both she and Mr. Williams decided to join me. When we arrived home next morning, most of our neighbours' houses had been bombed, and the air-raid shelter in Shepherds Bush had been destroyed by a land mine, causing a large number of fatalities. Not long after that incident I received a letter from Aunt Bess urging me to return home, for both she and mother were very concerned about me and were afraid that I might be killed in the air-raids.

Not long after receiving her letter, I decided that it was best for me to return home. During the war period I fell in love with a young man, Alban Mabe, who worked for the R.A.F. ground staff at Doncaster. When I was at home with mother, my boyfriend had some leave, and it was during his leave that he proposed to me, and in March, 1941, we got married. In the height of the War period my husband was moved to various R.A.F. stations around the country and naturally I followed him. On one occasion I had to return home since unfortunately, mother had become ill again. On my return I could see that she was gravely ill. About three weeks after my return home, on 10th October, 1942, she passed into the Higher Life. I loved my mother very much and naturally her death saddened me very deeply.

On the day of mother's funeral, I was summoned to appear before the Labour Tribunal, for not attending work. Mother's burial was at 11.00 a.m., coinciding with the time that I should have appeared before the tribunal. Although I tried to contact the tribunal to explain my tragic circumstances, I was unsuccessful. The day following mother's funeral I appeared before the tribunal to explain why I had not been able to attend work. At first I sensed their hostility toward me. But after I had explained my circumstances, I was told to start work the following week, working for the C.I.A.! . . . the Chief Inspector of Armaments at the Rhigos Works near Hirwaun, South Wales. My job involved the inspection of munitions.

In January, 1943, I became ill and unfit for work after suffering from an attack of gastric influenza. Two weeks later I went back to work to find that the bus that was detailed to return us home from work, was for some unknown reason no longer available to us. This meant that we workers had to wait around in the bitter cold at the end of our afternoon shift.

On making enquiries, I was told that our bus was being used to transport the night shift to their work stations instead of returning the afternoon workers to their homes. So the following day I went to the transport office to enquire of Mr. Ted ("Skip") Morgan what was happening to our bus. "Skip" was an honest, honourable man and he advised me to speak to his boss. After explaining the situation to his boss, as I turned to leave his office, I heard him say to

"Skip", "Let her try to do her damnedest!"

I turned to "Skip" and said, "That is exactly what I shall do. He has not heard the end of this!"

The next day I wrote to the Minister In Charge of War Transport and explained to him our predicament regarding the bus.

At that time I was a shop-stewardess for the Transport and General Workers' Union. Sometime after, as I was walking through the Rhigos plant with the Work's Convenor, together with the Chief Inspector, Mr. Darrant, Mr. Darrant turned to me and said, "I would give my right arm to find out who has been writing to the Ministry of Transport."

"You don't have to look far, it was me," I replied.

Little did I realise that my letter had stirred up a hornets' nest. Investigations later showed that although a factory bus had been designated to drive the night shift workers to their work stations, its allocation was not being used. Our afternoon bus was being used instead. This meant petrol from the night shift bus, allocated to drive the night shift to their work stations, was available to be siphoned off by some local managers for their private motor cars. At that time, Mr. Ernest Bevin was the Minister of Labour, and I was called before his committee to explain our predicament.

After the War I was unemployed for a few years, but in the mid 1950s I took up employment again in a factory known locally as the Perry Chain Works, which specialised in the manufacture of bicycle chains. During my period there my male colleagues had a football team but did not have a football field of their own. They asked me what could be done to raise funds for their football ground. I suggested that we could organise a Drama Society and use the attendance proceeds towards the purchase of a field. Consequently, I ended up producing Somerset Maughan's play, *The Sacred Flame*, from which we cleared about one hundred pounds profit, which in those days was a considerable sum of money.

I enjoyed working at the "Perry Chain" for about two and a half years, but unfortunately the work was dirty and greasy, forcing me to terminate my employment after suffering from dermatitis and urticaria, a condition which produced large weals on my arms.

In the early days of my marriage, my husband and I had a very happy relationship, but unknown to me at that moment, it was to be the beginning of my emotional suffering. Although I had endured much pain in my body, it did not compare with the suffering I had to undergo in my mind. At one time I was convinced that I was losing my sanity. My husband was continually levelling accusations against me that were completely false. I do not intend to reveal the exact nature of these accusations for I do not believe in revealing one's private life. However, it is sufficient to say that he continually invented false, hurtful stories about me. In turn, he used to torment me by saying that if I could not remember such an event, then I was losing my mind. Mentally he kept me on a knife-edge. In addition, he kept me very short of money and I had to account for every penny that I had spent. There were times when I had no money from him at all. Although I did not realise it at the time, he was withholding money from me so that he could spend it on his pleasures with other women. I was often hungry because I did not have enough money to buy food. Although he did not physically hit me, he often threatened me. This frightened me to such an extent that I clearly remember two occasions when I slept with a knife under my pillow. Events reached such a point that in 1947 we decided that we could not go on much longer and we separated. He found himself another woman, and in 1951 we ended up in the divorce court. I now realise that I had to go through such an emotional and financial experience so that I could help the numerous people who come to me today with their matrimonial problems.

Marian Butler (centre back) in costume in "Maids of the Mountain" with Oswald (Ossie) West (foreground).

16th December, 1964.

Dear Miss Butler,

    Please forgive me for having, through an oversight, omitted to write before now to acknowledge, with thanks, your letter to Lord Boothby of November 22nd. It reached me following his departure, on medical advice, for the West Indies for a long and complete rest. I passed your message on to him, and have no doubt he greatly appreciated your kind thought in writing.

    Yours sincerely,

Kathleen J. Taylor

Private Secretary to
Lord Boothby, K.B.E., LL.D.

Miss M. Butler,
28, Heol Maes-y-Dre,
Ystradgynlais,
Swansea.

A reply from Lord Boothby.

Chapter Three

THE HEALING GIFT

It was after my divorce, that I first became directly involved in healing. At first, my nephew Lyn was diagnosed by his doctor to be suffering from measles. However, the measle spots failed to develop and as a consequence, seemed to cause a kind of combustion within his body. This in turn lead to infantile convulsions, and he was later diagnosed as being epileptic. To say that he was suffering would be a great understatement of the truth, since at this particular stage of his illness he was experiencing grand and petit mal epileptic convulsions and would get them in what can be best described as 'cyclones'.

He would suffer as many as three hundred to three hundred and fifty convulsions over a weekend period. I knew this to be factual since Dr. Margaret Barry, who was attending Lyn, gave me a small notebook in which to record each convulsion. The doctor was very sympathetic with all of us who were attending to Lyn. Sometimes she would record as many as fifty or sixty convulsions during her visit. We took Lyn from place to place to try and find a cure for him, but to no avail. Finally it was agreed that we would take him to the Cardiff Royal Infirmary, to see a Professor Watkins.

When we first visited the Professor, he laughed me to scorn when I said that Lyn was having up to three hundred or three hundred and fifty convulsions over a weekend. He said that it was not possible. Of course I stressed to him these facts. Eventually, he decided to keep Lyn at the hospital for observation for a couple of weeks. When we later called to collect Lyn from the hospital, the Professor asked me to accept his profound apologies. During the time that he had been in hospital, they had recorded over one thousand convulsions.

When Lyn came home, he suffered greatly. At one particular time when we were nursing him, his little body became twisted. The local doctor was called to see what could be done for his tormented body. At this time Lyn was about two years and nine months old. When he had the epileptic attacks, it took as many as three adults to hold him down. Later he became so ill that he was given only a few months to live.

One particular day in March, 1950, I was in the bedroom with Lyn when I found my healing gift. I was always brought up to think that God was a God of Love. But how could a God of Love watch such a little boy suffer so much in this way? We had all been praying for God to make him better. But nothing happened. So we prayed that God would take Lyn from us, out of his pain and suffering. I said in a loud voice, "There cannot be a God, no God would do this!" I then remembered a book that my father had given me as a child, which I used to read in bed. The book was called *Christ my Saviour*. It was a small brown book with gold lettering. The book described the miracles of Jesus. I thought that this was the last straw. Then I shouted in a loud voice, "If only Christ was here. He could do something." A few seconds later, the bedroom door opened and a 'presence' entered the room. I cannot explain who or what it was. I never saw anyone or anything, I just felt a presence. The presence came past me, brushed my clothes and came between me and the little patient. I trembled from head to foot as the temperature in the room seemed to have plunged to zero. There seemed to be a high frequency etheric condition being generated in the bedroom. Of course, I did not realise it at the time, but a few minutes later when the presence seemed to have left the bedroom, the door clicked shut. The first thing that I did was to ask God to forgive me for having spoken as I did.

The door suddenly opened again, I was expecting a repeat performance of what had just happened, but it was my brother Ewart.

"Good God," said Ewart. "You look like you have seen a ghost."

"I have not seen one, but I have felt one," I replied.

"Don't be ridiculous. Look at the circumstances that you are in," said Ewart.

As he and I were talking, I happened to turn towards the bed and saw Lyn's lips move.

Since Lyn's last attack, in addition to his body being twisted, he had also become deaf, dumb, and blind. He was also completely spastic, unable to move his arms or his legs. I was totally surprised when his little lips moved. I knelt down beside him and forgetting that he was deaf, I asked him, "What do you want Darling?"

To my surprise Lyn said, "I want my Mammy."

I went down the stairs and called my sister-in-law to come up to the bedroom. She never questioned what had happened. She picked Lyn up into her arms, cuddled and caressed him. This scene of mother and her little child was a joy to behold. As I went downstairs, I was still very badly shaken. I picked up a shawl and returned to the bedroom, placed it around both mother and child, and left the room.

As soon as I had reached the bottom of the stairs, the front door opened and the doctor entered into our house, with a death certificate in her hand. All that was left to complete the form was for it to be signed and dated.

"You must be prepared for a shock, doctor," I said.

"It won't come as a shock to me," she replied. "I was here last night after I had visited a midwifery case and called back to see Lyn, I could see that his heart was failing fast."

She continued to explain by saying that it was her day off and she wanted to see the case through, since she was writing a thesis on epilepsy. Then she walked up the stairs, holding the death certificate in her hand. I remained in the hallway below. Suddenly she dropped her bag and said, "My God he can see!"

After that tremendous experience with Lyn, I felt very disturbed in my mind. Not disturbed in the sense that I did not know how to deal with this power. But, what was this power? Where did it come from? How was it being directed? Through prayer! Yes! But I knew in my mind that there was much more to it than that. I therefore decided to form a sympathetic group of people around me. I offered them the facility of coming to sit with me for one hour every week, for the sole purpose of finding out what this power was all about and how it came to be in our midst, and above all, how it was going to be used in my life. What had I done to release such an energy that I could not understand? Very kindly, eight people came to sit with me. None of these people had any knowledge about this work, other than they knew that I was sincere in my endeavours and that they wanted to help me.

Our 'sittings' commenced by entering into the 'silence'. I would open the proceedings with a prayer. In the opening prayer I would ask that our minds be opened so that we could understand what this power was and how it could be utilised. We would then all repeat the *Lord's Prayer* together and sit in silence for about one hour. Although we all had a wonderful time just sitting in the peaceful silence, nothing seemed to happen. This silence was always beautiful, however, sometimes we would listen to music or sing hymns. This same routine continued many times, until in one of our sittings I began to fall asleep. A deep, deep, peaceful sleep. Later I would awaken and feel very refreshed. My first reaction was to apologise to my co-sitters for having fallen asleep.

Things continued in this way, once a week for about six solid months. Then one evening when I awoke, I again apologised for having fallen asleep. One of my sitters turned to me in amazement and said, "Sleep! There has been an Indian Guide speaking through you for about half an hour. He said his name was White Eagle."

At this time there was much confusion in the minds of my sitters, for neither they nor I were conversant with the workings of the laws of Spirit Communication. The confusion was compounded by the fact that the name "White Eagle" was also associated with the White Eagle Lodge. This was mentioned to my Indian Guide when he spoke through me. He replied by saying, "You can call me by another name if you like. You can call me Raheede." Today I realise that the name "White Eagle" was a popular tribal name, in the same manner as David Jones is very popular today. Since that occasion over forty years ago, whenever I go into the trance state, Raheede has always spoken as my personal Spiritual Guide and Door-keeper. I have since discovered that Raheede was a member of the Cherokee nation and I have always found him to be a very dear friend whose friendship, love and guidance I will cherish to eternity.

Although I never had much schooling, I can honestly say that I have experienced life and the many different aspects that trouble people. How can we surmount these troubles? How can we help to unload the burdens of people who come to us for Healing? How can any human channel equate the depth of what has happened? Maybe the troubles were created in this life or they brought them into this life when they reincarnated; before they were born. During all these experiences, I have had a wonderful friend in Raheede. Many people will deny or argue about the words that I now write, however, my interpretation of Scripture has helped me reconcile many things.

When Jesus spoke to His Disciples when they were in fear of losing Him, they all wondered what was going to happen to them. They were afraid that they were going to lose the most wonderful Light that had entered into their lives. These are the words that Jesus said to them:

'Tarry ye in Jerusalem until the "Comforter" shall come and teach thee many things.'

Many, many theologians would dispute the facts, but they could never convince me otherwise, for I have proved Raheede to be a Comforter from Spirit, in every sense of the word. He has helped to unravel problems, he has helped to find missing persons, and has worked on many levels of understanding.

After my experience with Lyn's illness, I continued with healing at the little Sanctuary at my aunt's home at 28, Heol Maes-y-Dre, Ystradgynlais. After giving healing at a frequency of about two to three times a week without payment, I thought that it would only be right and proper that patients should pay something for what they had received. I did not want them to pay any money, since monetary payment never entered my head nor formed any part of healing. However, I decided to call some people together in the form of a thanksgiving, so that they could give thanks for what they had received. Every person to whom I spoke wanted to come to the service, I had no refusals.

Consequently it was about Easter time in 1950, that we held our first service in my aunt's home. We were about thirty in number. At the end of the service. I was asked if it would be possible to have another service in which my friend Mr. Oswald (Ossie) West was presiding. On this second occasion, we were about twenty in number. Again everyone said that they had enjoyed the service and it was suggested that we should in future, hold regular services. However, this was a development that would mean we would be imposing on the hospitality of my aunt, after all, it was her home.

At that time I was primarily a Trance Medium and often held regular circles with close friends. During one of these circles, the question of further circles at my aunt's home arose. Raheede said that he had no earthly home at which to hold such services and that he did not like to encroach on someone else's territory. At this point my aunt said:

"Raheede, you can have my home."

"You do not realise what you are saying, my sister," said Raheede.

"Oh yes I do," she replied. "You can have my home to operate in as long as I have enough space for myself in the small back room, and I have my own bedroom and of course the bathroom, you can have the rest of my home."

That is how the Temple of Light Church first started, and it was

Raheede who gave the church its full name:

THE TEMPLE OF LIGHT CHURCH
AND INDEPENDENT
CHRISTIAN SPIRITUAL HEALING SANCTUARY

We held regular services at the house until we built our new church which was opened on the 14th April, 1987. Raheede made a number of stipulations, one was that healers should wear white coats. (At that time I did not realise what he meant about white coats.) Raheede also said that since we were going to hold regular services at my aunt's home, we should all make an offering. No one was under any obligation to give, but he said that he would be grateful for anything that could be given. He also told us to open a bank account in the name of the Temple of Light Church. From that day we have not looked back and fortunately our little church has grown from strength to strength.

Through the church, I have known very many eminent people in the Healing movement, such as Maurice Barbanell, who was editor of the publications *Psychic News* and *Two Worlds*. Maurice was a great exponent of the Healing movement. I have also associated with Harry Edwards, the world-renowned Spiritual Healer, who did more for Spiritual Healing than anyone I know. I also knew Gordon Turner, he too was also a very great expander of the spiritual truth and has done tremendous work for the Healing movement. During my life I have met many of the leading mediums in the country, many of whom have been to my home.

After the church was formed, and not long after my first experience with Lyn, I was asked to visit a woman who was the landlady of a public house. I was told that she had had a cerebral haemorrhage. Her left arm was paralysed, also she could hardly stand, and walking was an impossibility for her. It was on a winter's afternoon when I decided to visit her. It was around midday and snow had just started to fall upon the ground. As the afternoon progressed, the snow carpeted the ground, growing ever deeper. In turn, I grew more apprehensive about visiting her. This apprehension was due to the fact that I had a hole in my shoe and I was concerned that I would get my foot wet, which could possibly result in a cold or flu. Since I had suffered so much in my early life, I was always mindful of the fact that I should protect my body the best I could. As I could not afford to have the shoes repaired, I placed a few layers of cardboard in the sole of my shoe to cover the hole. However, I decided that it was unwise to visit the lady in such adverse weather conditions. I telephoned her and explained to her that I could not make the appointment, but I suggested to her that she should "send out her thoughts" and ask for help. At the same time I would pray for her in the sanctuary at my aunt's home.

After I had prayed for her, there was a knock at the front door, and as I opened the door, I found it was my brother Ewart. He explained to me that another lady wanted to come to see me. He said that I had helped her many years before, on the occasion when she had lost her purse on the way to Swansea. I recollected that she wanted to get off the bus to search for her purse. Instead, I lent her a ten-shilling-note (50p today) for her bus fare. She eventually moved away from the locality and we lost contact with each other. Ewart continued to explain that this lady was returning to Ystradgynlais for a holiday, during which she wanted to take the opportunity of repaying the money she had borrowed many, many years before. This lady visited me and repaid the money that she had borrowed, which enabled me to have my shoes repaired. The cost of the repairs amounted to nine shillings and eleven pence. The one penny change I have kept to this day. It serves to remind me of how poor I was and how fortunate I was to have my shoes repaired. Although there were many times when I was on the brink of being almost destitute, some money always seemed to turn up to help me out of my financial difficulties. Although I have endured much suffering in my life, I can honestly say that I have also experienced some of life's treasures, many that cannot ever be financially valued.

One case springs to mind which serves to illustrate some of the events that began to happen in my life. A lady came to see me and explained that her daughter had been missing from home for two days. She had already asked the police to form a search-party, but they advised her to wait one more day and to come to see me to establish if I could be of any assistance. When she arrived she began to cry almost instantly. At the same time the word "Canterbury" came into my mind.

I asked her, "Does the name Canterbury mean anything to you?"

"It does not mean a thing to me, I don't even know anyone in Canterbury," she replied.

"Can you please find my missing daughter," she sobbed.

"Yes," I replied. "Canterbury must be an important link. Do you have any relatives or friends in Canterbury?"

"No," she emphatically replied. As she answered, I had the sensation of a hard, fist-like blow hitting me to the side of my chin. This left the impression on my mind that her daughter might have hung herself! I associated the fist-like blow to be a knot in the rope. Of course I kept this information to myself. Nevertheless, the word "Canterbury" and the blow to my chin kept on recurring over and over again in my mind. Since I did not seem to be making much progress, I eventually forced these impressions out of my mind. I told the mother that I would continue to pray for her daughter's safety and well-being.

Two days later, the same lady returned to see me with joy written all over her face, as her daughter had returned home. She informed me how her daughter had disappeared. At first, the girl had hitch-hiked to Canterbury. She arrived there penniless and without anywhere to stay. She was destitute, so she visited the Salvation Army Hostel. I then realised that the knot under the right-hand side of my chin related to the Salvation Army bonnets that are worn by its female members. My Guides had been trying to communicate this information to me. (Today, my communication with the Guides is generally much clearer. Often it is in the form of a clear picture, clairvoyantly, or in the form of sound, clairaudiently. Very often, I find that I can converse quite naturally with my Guides.) When the Salvation Army had discovered what the girl had done, they returned her home to her parents. The Salvation Army returned her to Brecon and from there, the police escorted her home.

The satisfaction of knowing that the information that the Guides had been trying to communicate to me was correct, gave me a deep sense of personal joy. This experience began to address some of the negative experiences that I had lived through. Such events enabled me to acquire vast reservoirs of knowledge. Such knowledge I could not have learned from school or from others. Over the years I consider myself to have been very fortunate to have received such information. Information on how to heal the sick, how to relieve pain, and information about how life goes on in Spirit. Also I learnt how to counsel on the numerous matters that affect people in their daily lives. Such knowledge has been passed on to others who have in turn passed it on to others and so on. That is how the word about my work has spread. This in turn has lead to my own spiritual growth. Just as it was recorded in Scripture:

'A sower went forth to sow.'

In my particular case, I feel as if a bag of seeds had been placed in my hands to spread in the vineyards of the unkown. I also feel that a tremendous amount of spiritual growth resulted from these seeds, from which spiritual branches could grow, similar to that which is recorded in the book of Revelations:

'For the healing of the nations, they should come and sit on the branches of the trees.'

I feel that with my colleagues, we have created similar spiritual branches. At this stage I would like to pay tribute to those colleagues who have worked with me over the years. In the early days, both Desmond (Des) Bennett and Oswald (Ossie) West were a tremendous help to me. I would also like to acknowledge the devotion of my niece, Gwenda Jones, we have worked together for almost forty years. Despite their help and that of many others, I feel that as yet, we have not fully realised the full potential of Spiritual Healing. We are only beginning to realise that disease can be alleviated by music, colour, and in many other different ways. I feel we are only just touching the fringes of the many forms of dynamic energies that are available which could help us overcome all sorts of maladies and illness that exist on our Earth Planet.

Today, I think my deepest joy is experienced when I am able to communicate with my Spirit Guides, who are able to inform me of the precise cause of the disease. Before a perfect cure can be brought about the cause or causes must first be removed. When the Spirit Guides are able to produce such information, at first the patient very often cannot accept the diagnosis or cannot remember the event that caused the illness in the first place. For example, I may have been informed by the Guides that the patient had fallen downstairs or had had an injury to his or her back. Quite often the patient cannot recall the event, but his wife or mother will often remember. However, when the patient is able to recall such an event, I know that I am on the right road to success.

At this stage I would like to explain who gives me such information. As you know, my main Guide, Door-keeper and very dear friend, is Raheede. He has informed me that in total he has access to about a further two hundred Guides who work with him. They come from all walks of life; nurses, doctors, bankers, lawyers, etc. However, I would like to point out that my main Healing Guide is Dr. Clive Osborne, who was an eye specialist and lived in Essex when on the Earth Plane. Very often it is Dr. Osborne who is able to make the diagnosis and who is able to explain how the disease was caused in the first instance. The disease may have been caused by an accident, or be due to environmental conditions, it may be of a psychosomatic origin or even a congenital condition. The cause of the disease can be multifarious. Another of the medical Guides who works through me is Dr. John Peters, he was a Paediatrician by profession. I am not always able to communicate with him directly, but through Raheede I know that he is never very far away from me. There are also other doctors; a Dr. Graham Moffat and Dr. Karl Hoffman. The latter was an Austrian who uses me in all cancer cases. In the early stages of my mediumship I was also close to Edith Cavell. She was shot at dawn in 1915, the year of my birth, for helping allied forces during the First World War. Although she still works with my band of Guides, I do not receive direct communication from her today. In more recent years I am given information that enables me to obtain a diagnosis far more quickly than I was able to in the early days of my mediumship.

Today the field of Spiritual Healing is becoming more dynamic. This is also true of traditional medicine of course. I hold traditional medicine in high esteem. However, as the waiting lists for traditional medicine grow ever longer, and fewer and fewer people can afford private treatment, I feel that this will allow the work of God to come even more to the forefront. These adverse economic circumstances will present the patient with the opportunity to seek Spiritual Healing. In general, there is no charge for Spiritual Healing, however, all free will donations are always gratefully accepted for the upkeep of the church, for its heating bills, etc. At the Temple of Light Church, none of the healers get paid. Those who are healed should also be grateful to God for that which they have received from God. They should also be aware of the needs of others and be prepared to render service when required to do so. No matter how the reader will evaluate Spiritual Healing, I will always unbiasedly rate it first class and second to no other treatment. The Lord Jesus was of course the great Master Healer who could heal by faith, by touch with the 'Laying on of Hands', and even by thought. The more that the healers and the public realise this, the more they will grow Spiritually. In my opinion, there is no known disease that cannot respond to Spiritual Healing to some degree. It is not always possible to effect a complete cure, but in my experience, Spiritual Healing always leads to an improvement in the health state. In opposition to my opinion, there are those who think that Spiritual Healers are only deluding themselves. Those who propound such opinions do not either understand or fully appreciate the scope of Spiritual Healing. Often it has been said to me, "I think that I have done my best for so and so, but he died!" When people think in this way, it is one of their biggest misunderstandings. The healing has not failed. Quite often there was no way possible for a healing to take place, after all Spiritual Healing cannot overcome the natural laws that govern us all. However, when they do pass on into the Higher Life, they are relieved of their suffering. There are also those people who think that they can live on the Earth Plane without God. Very often they too turn to Him in adversity. In the course of my healing work I have met many atheists and agnostics who have come to see me in their depths of despair. They do not believe in God or know how to find him, yet they want to seek his help! Similarly they are not prepared to change their views but still seek his help. In such circumstances, I think this gives the healing channels the opportunity to transmit the love and compassion of God to them.

Through the development of the church we progressed both spiritually and physically, we became more and more involved with people and their illnesses. One occasion was of particular interest to me. It happened one Friday evening when a woman came to see me in the Sanctuary. Normally I commenced healing at about 2.00 p.m. and I would carry on until about 8.30 p.m. It was a very memorable day. It started with me escorting a lady to see our local dental surgeon, for a tooth to be extracted. Although she was highly nervous about this, I could not really understand this, since I had suffered so much as a child, that the extraction of a tooth gave me no fear whatsoever. Before we left for the surgery I became aware that I was walking into a gloomy situation. I seemed to be surrounded with gloom and despair, but I did not realise what it was all about. I was not told anything or given any indication whatsoever. It was just my sensitivity reacting to the situation.

The lady eventually had her tooth extracted. I escorted her out of the surgery and she went home by bus, and I walked home alone. After I had reached home, I turned the television on and suddenly there was a news flash about the Aberfan disaster which had just occurred on that fateful Friday of the 21st October, 1966. Although I continued with my healing work in the afternoon, the memory of which remains vivid in my mind to this day, the longer that I worked at healing, the more I felt that I was burning myself up. Finally, I felt as though I had a raging furnace inside of me. Although I had an evening healing clinic to do, I felt that I could not carry on anymore. I became very much aware of those poor souls who had died during the disaster and had become Earth-bound. They did not realise that they had remained in the gloom, darkness and despair where they were.

I said to the people who had gathered for my evening clinic, "I am very sorry, I cannot continue to give you healing. I have got to do something for those poor souls or I think that my body will burst."

"What do you mean?" they asked.

"I have got to get people together to pray," I replied.

Consequently, I broke off the evening clinic and I made a telephone call to the local minister of the Congregational Church, the Rev. Arfon Lewis. His wife answered the telephone and said that her husband had gone out to visit members of his parish. However, she said that he would return my call as soon as he returned home. Within approximately half an hour he contacted me. I informed him that I thought that we should hold a prayer meeting for those poor people who had just died at Aberfan.

"What do you expect me to do?" he asked. "Shall we hold a meeting in your house?"

"No," I replied. "My home will be much too small, especially when the crowds start to arrive."

"What do you expect to happen?" enquired the minister.

"I don't know, but expect a lot of people to come," I replied.

"How can we contact people? It is past 7.00 p.m. and the hour is already late," said the minister.

"It is never too late to hold a prayer meeting," I said

He agreed.

"If you get off the telephone quickly, I will contact all the local clergy to see if anything can be arranged. I will get back to you as soon as I can," said the minister.

He was true to his word. They decided to hold a service in the vestry of the local chapel called "Sardis" at 9.00 p.m. Each minister in turn contacted members of their own denomination. I in turn, asked my Niece Gwenda to join me. We travelled in her car and on the way to "Sardis" I was overcome with emotion. I stopped everyone that we met on our way and said to them, that if they were concerned about the people who had been killed in Aberfan, then they should join us at the service. Naturally everyone said that they were concerned, consequently they joined us. On our way we collected my brother Ewart who was a Presenter of the Congregational Church Choir. I asked him to join us. He replied by saying that if a service had been arranged then he would have known about it.

"No you don't," I said. We have only just organised it in the last hour."

We arrived at the vestry and it was packed with people. I asked the people of the congregation to channel their thoughts towards those poor children who had died so tragically so that their souls could be handed over to God. Frankly, I thought that they did not know much about this kind of work. However, through my mediumistic powers, I was able to enlighten them. We all sat in silence, translating our thoughts so that these poor little souls could be given over to their Maker and our Lord Jesus Christ.

I will never forget that occasion. It was a wonderfully moving service. There was an awe and a tremendous feeling of responsibility about it. We felt that we had become the custodians of those poor little souls who had passed on. We felt as if we were handing them over one by one to their Maker in the Higher Life. It was a very memorable day for me and many others. A day I will never forget.

Marian Butler.

Marian Butler with Harry Edwards at a N.F.S.H. Annual Dinner.

Chapter Four

CONFLICT

There are all types of people in the world whose behaviour in many, many ways is analogous to the animals. Firstly, God made the Lion who is king of the jungle. This is the ferocious type of person. These types are always around and about us, consequently, we must always be on our guard against them. God also created the Tiger. This type of person is often found snarling and growling at others and just like the Tiger, which is always on the prowl, this type of person is always looking for retribution. He also created the beautiful, humble type of animal such as the deer. This type of person is almost always pleasant but is always vulnerable to the attack of the Lion or Tiger. There are also those types of person who are like the spiders or scorpions, they are always on the move here and there, tearing their way through life, always at the double and wasting their energies. This latter type will often say to me, "I don't want to die, but can you give me a quick healing for I have to catch the next bus."

In contrast you have the Turtle types of this world, they will get there some day. They don't care when, but they will get there eventually, and invariably live to a ripe old age. There are also the Doves of this world; the peaceful type of person who always brings tranquillity to all who are about him. Conversely, you also have the Cuckoos, who are too lazy to do anything for themselves, they don't even build their own nests, but are always ready to pinch, steal, and ride on the efforts of others. This type is always on the lookout for the spoils, they are always 'on the take' and almost always want to exploit others when they are in adversity. During my life, I can honestly say that I have met almost all types of people.

After the emotional and financial trauma of my divorce, I found myself being ridiculed by the public at large and some were even quite hostile toward me. I realised that I would either have to throw in the towel or learn to become stronger so as to be able to fight further battles. I found that by continuing to fight I developed a tremendous armoury, which was my will and personal resolve. I said to myself that I had as much right to do what I wanted to do, as much right as those who wanted to oppose my work. They had no right to stop me from doing the things that God had wanted me to do.

In the early 1960s, when I was working at the local Smith's watch factory in the Enfield Works at Ystradgynlais, one of my colleagues accidentally mentioned that she did not have a birth certificate. I found this very strange for I knew that she could have obtained one from Somerset House. When I informed her of this fact she told me that she had not been born in the U.K., but Madras, in India. She explained that she had tried to obtain a certificate through the Commonwealth Office and also the Foreign Office. She had tried almost everywhere, but to no avail.

Since her father was in the twilight of his life, I advised her very strongly that she should obtain a birth certificate. If he died she would have no one to verify her birth or country of origin.

"Would you like me to get a copy of your birth certificate?" I asked.

"What could you do different to what I have done," she retorted.

"I could do it through the power of the Spirit, and I could write to Mr. Pandit Nehru if you like?"

I asked for the particulars of her mother, her name and time of birth, etc. In due course I composed a letter and posted it to Mr. Pandit Nehru, the Prime Minister of India. Four months passed before I received a reply through Mr. Nehru's Secretary. The letter explained that not long after my colleague was born, there had been terrible flooding in that region of Madras, resulting in the loss of most records, including the lady's birth certificate and those of many others. In addition, many thousands had drowned. Another four months passed by before I received a second letter from Mr. Nehru stating that the lady, Mrs. Ivy Bowen, nee Sutton, should go to Swansea and visit the Commissioner of Oaths Office. I was to instruct her to take a copy of this second letter with her, whereupon she could obtain a sworn affidavit that would confirm her date of birth and country of origin. Unfortunately, I have long lost contact with Mrs. Sutton and I do not know to this day if she did obtain the birth certificate that she had long searched for. After all my efforts, this was naturally a disappointment to me.

Through many struggles, I found myself growing taller spiritually. I found that I needed all my will, determination and spirituality to fight my next battle for personal survival. This battle also occurred during the time when I was doing 'piece work' at the Enfield watch factory. My work involved polishing watch bezels, which was a very dirty job. On this particular day, I found myself late for work, as unfortunately, I had overslept. When I eventually arrived at my work bench, it was just in time for our normal tea-break. The tea-lady was actually in the act of bringing the tea around to us. The ringing of the works' bell was a sign to all of us to get our purses ready to buy tea and refreshments. Suddenly, one of the girls said that she had had her purse stolen. I did not know at this time, but one of the other girls had put the purse into my pocket, and as I went to retrieve my purse, I noticed that I had picked up a strange purse and, quite innocently, I took it to the charge-hand and asked him if this was the one that had been reported missing. In turn, he asked the girl if it was hers. "Yes," she replied.

"Where did you get it from?" asked the charge-hand.

"In my pocket," I replied.

With the utterance of those words I sensed that I had already been found guilty, ready to be lynched before another word could be spoken. Someone had wanted to brand me a 'Spiritual Healing Thief'. Naturally, this made me feel terrible, even though I knew I was innocent. Even though the Guides took me to the brink of my endurance, fortunately, they rescued me. That experience was another tremendous shock in my life. Shortly, I found that the whole factory was against me. Can you imagine how I felt, the indignation of being stared at by about six hundred people whenever I left my work-station. Once again, I realised that I would either fold under that kind of psychological pressure or stand up and fight. After all I was not guilty of any wrong-doing.

What I am certain about is that I could not have fought that battle alone. I was only able to sustain my personal fight with the help of my Guides. I always felt my dear friends Ebernazin and Raheede close to me. As I left the factory each day, I realised that even my closest friends had deserted me. Everyone believed that I was a thief, they had no faith in me. For almost one solid month, I was 'sent to Coventry'. No one spoke to me, I was totally ostracised. Paradoxically, as time progressed, I did not seem to care that they thought wrongly of me, for I was able to enjoy the deep, rich companionship of my Guides, who stood close to me throughout the working day. At the end of this hurtful fiasco, the silence was finally broken by one of my colleagues and it was eventually decided that I should be given a second chance. Personally, I found it very difficult to give up this silence for I had experienced a wonderful month of solitude with my Guides. There had been nothing to disturb this silence, only the systematic rhythm of the machinery that worked around me.

Sometime later, I travelled afar, seeking contact with various mediums to see if they could establish if my good name would ever be cleared. I also became involved with the use of the pendulum, Radiesthesia. I have found the pendulum to be a very simple, yet very accurate tool, if it is used in the correct way, with the right mind, and above all, the right sincerity of purpose. It should never be used as a plaything, but if used sincerely, it can give genuine help and strength, and will always come up with the correct answers. So, one evening I decided that I would use the pendulum to establish the names of those who had wrongly accused me. I listed all the names of the people who had worked with me in the three various departments that I had worked in. Eventually, the same name kept recurring. In fact the pendulum pin-pointed the same name eleven times in succession. The same result was always achieved even though I placed the names on a piece of paper, face downwards, thus preventing me from consciously influencing the action of the pendulum in any way. The pendulum also came up with a second name, that of the accomplice who actually saw the purse being placed in my pocket. These two people kept their silence about this incident for three years. However, I was informed by my Guides that my name would be cleared before I would finish my term of employment at the factory, and it was! I shall never forget that incident in my life. Only those people who are innocent know what it is like to be wrongly accused. One has to tread that path before one can fully appreciate what it feels like. Unless one undergoes such experiences, one will never know what such deep suffering feels like.

In the early days of my Healing Ministry, people would come to Ystradgynlais, but would have difficulty in finding where I lived. Consequently, they would knock on neighbours' doors and ask where I lived. Many would reply by saying that they did not know me and that they certainly did not know where I lived. Many of my neighbours did not want to recognise me or my work. Both the local baker and milkman refused to serve me. In order to live I had to ask friends to buy milk and bread for me. That is how tough things had become. Although I was literally fed up to the teeth, I decided that I had to do something about it. Even though people had difficulty in finding my Sanctuary, they still came. However, I wanted to overcome the difficulty of locating the Sanctuary. I therefore asked the local Registrar if I could apply to Somerset House in London for permission to place a name-plate on the wall outside the front door of the Sanctuary. The plate would enable patients to find me more readily without being a source of aggravation to anyone. Even obtaining the name-plate turned out to be difficult, for Somerset House asked many questions. What were my intentions? What kind of work did I do? What were my inspirations? After about two years I was eventually given permission to hang the name-plate outside my Sanctuary. I was very proud of the words written upon that bronze plate:

THE TEMPLE OF LIGHT
SPIRITUAL HEALING SANCTUARY

Often when I returned home from working in the local watch factory, I could see the bronze plate shining in the reflection of the afternoon sun. It made me feel very proud indeed. Not long after I had had the plate secured and safely screwed to the wall, the factory closed down for its annual summer holiday. As a consequence, I informed my patients that I would be available to give them healing during the day as well as the night, at least for the following two weeks. But one afternoon, I heard a heavy knock on my front door. As I opened the front door, I was confronted by nine men, who had hammers and chisels at hand, ready to remove my bronze plate.

One of the men said, "We have come to remove the plate."

I replied, "Gentlemen, nine men against one woman, don't be ridiculous. If you want to take down the plate, I can't stop you. But when you remove that last screw from that plate, don't blame me if your arms become paralysed. God help you. You are waging war on the Almighty. You have attacked his work at every step and he is not going to tolerate you any longer. The choice is yours. What are you going to do?"

One man started looking at the other. Suddenly, one man began to walk away, then another, and then another, until finally only one man was left standing at my door. Then he too finally walked away.

Eventually, it was I who removed that plate, just after my new Church was built on the land opposite my home. As I removed the plate, I asked God not to paralyse my arms for I explained that I was taking it down for good. I still have that original name-plate, and today it serves to remind of the many events that we experienced together. Many times it had been painted over by various people of different religious beliefs. It has been tarred, daubed with human excreta, and defaced many times, but each time I was able to wash it clean.

The new Church was built in 1987 and it continues to grow from strength to strength. The numerous objectors have now ceased. I am very proud of the Church and I am certain that it will continue to grow long after my life on the Earth Plane has ended. Therefore, I firmly believe that mediums are tested. I have spoken to many in my life and I have always found this to be true.

Even today, I still find myself being tried and tested by Spirit, but now the tasks are not so great or so frequent. However, I still have some enemies and some live quite near to me, but I will not reveal their names. But the day will eventually come when they will alter their way of thinking, be it in this world or the next. I still wish them all the best that life has to offer and that they may continue to enjoy happiness and blessings. One thing I do know, they will never enjoy the happiness that I experience as I work in the Church with those whom I care for. Eventually, everyone responds to the power of love.

Animals too, respond to the power of love; love is always easily understood. I have healed many of my friends in the animal kingdom; cats, dogs, horses, cows, and sheep. Everything that I have done with Spirit has been very important to my own spiritual growth. I shall never forget those times and I hope that I shall gather more such treasures as life goes on. I hope too that I shall be able to share them with others.

At the time when the Sanctuary was being established, it brought me into conflict with the public, particularly with those members of my own town of Ystradgynlais. The local people used to go out of their way to make my life unbearable. Today when I look back, I understand why they were doing that. They must have thought that I was bringing a demonic source into their midst and that this in turn would have serious repercussions on their own spiritual growth. However, my intentions were only to bring more enlightenment and the physical involvement of true spiritual matters. They would then have the opportunity to evaluate the true Christian teachings for themselves.

After the Sanctuary had become established there followed my involvement with the press. There were many different types of newspapers which were involved in my work – *The Herald of Wales*, *Western Mail* and the *Evening Post*. However, there was one particular occasion when the local newspaper, *The South Wales Labour Voice*, produced an article on my work, which continued for many months. It began when a local reporter came to see for herself what was going on. She used to ask many questions. One day she decided to carry on this debate in the local newspaper. This in turn brought tremendous interest about my work to the general public and as a consequence, the sales of our local newspaper increased considerably. Unfortunately, when I replied to the reporter's questions or comments, I never had a fair opportunity to reply. She was able to write, sometimes up to half a page, whereas my reply was often condensed into a few lines of print. Of course, this meant my replies often did not make much sense at all to the readers.

I really thought that I was fighting a losing battle. Or was I? Was I fighting this losing battle only to win the bigger battle in the end? After all, I had been torn to shreds and ridiculed so much by the press. This also led to verbal abuse being hurled at me by the readers. This made me realise that this fight was meant to be, and I had to fight with all my might. After all, I was in possession of some vital information that very few people had. For example, during one occasion when I was 'sitting', it coincided with the period when the American astronauts were being launched into space.

Suddenly the Guides said: "They are in trouble now, and there is not much that they can do about it themselves."

Within a few days of the Guide uttering this statement, it was confirmed in the press that some astronauts had been in serious difficulties. However, at that time, neither my name nor my involvement in this matter was ever publicly released. However, this event proved to me that I was in touch with reality, and not as some people tended to think, that I was dealing with something that was obscure, or intangible which did not make much sense. The more that I became involved in this work, the deeper I was being led into wider avenues of understanding. These events of course, attracted many kinds of different people; theologians, doctors, nurses, judges, etc. It can be seen that during that period in my life I was really fighting a supreme battle, for my survival.

It must be remembered that in those early days, the Witchcraft Act of 1603 was still in existence for it was not until 1951 that it was eventually repealed. In fact the famous medium Helen Duncan, who was a physical medium, was imprisoned for her beliefs. Consequently, in my early spiritual circles the local Constabulary used to sit in with me to ensure that everything was proper and to ensure that I was not dabbling in any 'Witchcraft'. In total, they sat in with me on about twenty to thirty occasions. Eventually I had a very good rapport with the police. They finally departed when one of the police constables who had injured his back, had it treated by me, and when his condition improved, the police did not bother me anymore. I assume that it was personal testimony to the fact that I was not practising Witchcraft!

Later my colleagues and I became members of the National Federation of Spiritual Healers at the time when Harry Edwards was President. My colleagues at that time were my niece, Gwenda Jones, and Oswald (Ossie) West, who is now deceased. We were all regular members at seminars and summer schools organised by the N.F.S.H. It was during this period that we, in our own right, became recognised healers. In 1950, I was Secretary of the Welsh Healers Association within the N.F.S.H. and we used to hold regular monthly meetings and services with the Rev. Leon Atkin in the Spiritualist Church in Swansea. At one of these meetings we agreed to invite Harry Edwards to give a public demonstration at the Brangwyn Hall, Swansea. Harry Edwards agreed, and he and his colleagues, Olive and George Burton, gave that public demonstration during the Whitsun holidays of 1962. There were also many other renowned healers there from most parts of the country including Hampshire and Dorset, Sussex, Essex, the Greater London and the Greater World Associations. The Healing Demonstration took place in the afternoon. Also taking part in the service was the Pontardulais mixed choir, conducted by Mr. Haydn Thomas. As is well known, Harry Edwards used to sit in a physical circle with Mr. Jack Webber, the famous Welsh medium. Prior to each sitting they used to sing the Welsh Hymn, *Calon Lan*. Coincidentally, the same hymn was sung that afternoon. I felt very proud when Harry Edwards told me he was grateful for the spiritual feast that I had organised.

In December, 1960, I received a letter from Harry Edwards asking me to represent the N.F.S.H. before the Cardiff Hospital Management Committee. Healer members of the N.F.S.H. had previously been given permission to attend patients in the Cardiff hospital region. However, for some unknown reason this permission had been withdrawn. Harry Edwards did not approve of this action, since he felt that the patients would lose out. When I went before the management committee that day, I felt that I was like Daniel walking into the Lions' den. I sensed that the whole committee, some thirty to forty members, were all against me. I felt that I was fighting for the very existence of the N.F.S.H. I was asked many questions that day, but I felt that one question in particular was most crucial. I was asked if I could cite a case where Spiritual Healing had succeeded where medical science had failed. At first, I replied by saying that I preferred to answer the question in a private session. I knew that the questioner had been one of the doctors who had treated my nephew, Lyn, when he was suffering so terribly from epilepsy. However, I was pressed to give my answer in the open session. I therefore cited the case of my nephew, Lyn. I assured the doctor that Lyn was still alive, despite the fact that originally he had been given only a few more weeks to live. I could see the look of disbelief on his face. After I had given my answer, the chairman asked for an adjournment in the proceedings. I realised that they wanted time to check out my story.

In January, 1961, I received a letter from the Secretary of the Cardiff Hospital Management Committee, Stanley Barry, which stated that the Management Committee had by a narrow majority, agreed to continue with the permission previously granted to healers of the N.F.S.H. to attend patients in the Cardiff hospitals.

Despite the harassment of the public and the press, many events occurred which filled me with happiness and lifted me above the pettiness of mankind. For example, on the same day as the American President, J. F. Kennedy, was assassinated, Aunt Bess and I were sitting in the back room of the Sanctuary when I heard the cry of a cat. I went out of the room, but I could not see any sign of the cat. The second time I heard a cry, and on searching, I found a cat cowering under the window-sill of the Sanctuary. As I approached it, I could see it was heavily blood-stained underneath. Closer examination revealed that its stomach had been torn open, with a wound of about six inches long, possibly caused by barbed-wire. The wound was so severe that the intestines were almost hanging from its body. I eventually coaxed the cat into the hallway and gave it some Spiritual Healing. When I returned from the back room to dress the wound with a bandage, the cat had disappeared. However, at about the same time the following day, the cat returned. It maintained this ritual for seven consecutive days and every time it appeared I gave it healing. On the seventh day the cat was completely healed and found sufficient confidence to enter my Sanctuary, and was finally found standing before my shrine, which comprised of a cross and a picture of Christ above it, as if it was saying, "Thank you for my healing." Such simple yet spectacular events to me, sustained and reminded me of the fact that what I was doing was worthwhile. Even to this day, I do not know to whom the cat belonged.

This event also proved to me that if a cat can be healed, then faith in God is not essential for Spiritual Healing to take effect. However I do believe that faith in God is an important aspect of healing, but it is not essential. Since those early days I have healed many animals, babies, and even atheists.

Sometime later I heard a light knock on the Sanctuary door and on opening it, I found a little girl of about four to five years of age, cradling a broken doll in her arm, sobbing her little heart out. "Can you heal my dolly please?" she asked.

"Yes," I replied.

As she handed me the doll I could see that its arms were broken. I thought to myself, "Can I repair the doll?" I quickly realised what to do.

"I think your dolly will have to stay here overnight. Trust me and come back again tomorrow morning at about 11 o'clock. By then she should be better. If not, you can come and visit her again."

After the child left, I took the doll to a local blacksmith to see if he could repair the doll's arm. He quickly replaced the doll's arm back in its socket, and the doll was as good as new again. The following morning the little girl returned and was pleased to find that her little doll had been healed.

She kissed me and said, "Thank you."

About two hours later she returned with a daisy-chain, which she placed in front of my shrine. Such happy, simple incidents will always remain in my memory.

Although I had caught the imagination of the press regarding the things that I was 'seeing', I can remember that during this conflict, there were some very happy, glorious times. Although the press wanted to see me kicked around, their words were never enough to injure me. Later it came about that I was invited to take part on television. This again was another experience! There was more ridicule and mockery of my beliefs. They wanted to put me down even more than the press had previously done. The things that were said about me angered me beyond belief, more than words can explain. I felt that the T.V. people were not only trying to belittle me but were also ridiculing God. They were trying to trespass on, what to me was, His really beautiful territory. I felt that they should never have been allowed to do what they had done to me. In my own mind, I can equate these events with some of those events that Jesus and His Disciples had to experience when they lived on the Earth Plane. Both He and His disciples had to fight all the way to bring light into the world. They too had to experience ridicule, but my ridicule was nothing to compare with that which they had to endure. My feelings were just as irate against the injustice, and angered me as much as it did the Disciples. I am quite sure of that. I felt that they could not have felt worse than I did at that particular time.

After many a long and hard battle, the press in general was won over and became far less hostile towards me and my work. Eventually, I decided that I would bring my conflict with the local press to a happy conclusion. I did this by challenging the local reporter to a public debate. I suggested that the debate should take place in any hall as large or as small as they liked. I told them that an entrance fee would be charged, which would be donated to a charity of their choosing. I said that I did not want to be associated with any monies that would be gained from the debate. In addition, I felt that the debate would give a very good opportunity for me to present my case. I felt sure there would not have been a local hall large enough to hold all the people who were likely to attend. But I was denied even this opportunity, since the reporter was not prepared to accept my challenge. Although the debate did not take place, it did do some good, since it prevented me from wasting any more of my time, and the matter was brought to a close. I realised that all I was achieving was to increase the sales of the newspaper. At the same time, my replies had been reduced to a few lines only. Eventually, I wished the newspaper and its readers a very happy Christmas and stated that if ever any of them felt the need of help, enlightenment or healing, it would be my privilege to help them.

Although that was the end of the story as far as the local press was concerned, it did not end my involvement with television. When the events with the press stopped, events with television continued. During that period of time I was interviewed by the B.B.C., B.B.C. Wales, T.W.W., and H.T.V. Again, there were many, many things that were said that were derogatory. However, I realised that no matter what was said against me, I was certain that the truth that I had spoken would prevail in the end. Eventually even the hardened T.V. interviewers became less hostile.

As my schoolteacher used to say, "If what you did was blessed by God, you would succeed, if not, you would remain in damnation for the rest of your life."

At least I am not in damnation, so I feel that I must have done some good!

During my life I have been very fortunate to meet people from all walks of life and of all casts and creeds, I have also been in contact with people of the criminal world. My heart goes out to those unfortunate people, who even though they have often broken both the natural and criminal law of the land, very often too are victims. They are victims of being unloved and unwanted, often denied the basics of life that we all need. I feel that if I had not become involved in healing, I would have liked to have worked in the Prison Service. I feel there must be some special spot for those less fortunate people in my heart. I do not condone their wrong-doings, I would never do that, however, I feel very strongly that in many cases, they should be shown more compassion. Many of course, would not agree with me.

One criminal who came to see me for Spiritual Healing had been punished with the Cat-o'-nine tails. I've never seen such a mess on a person's back in all my life. Could I deny him the 'Laying on of Hands'? Could I deny him the love of God? I advised him that before he could receive the best from God he would have to make his own apologies to God for his wrong-doings to others. One should never deny God's help to anyone in their hour of need.

Today the ridicule of neighbours, doctors, nurses, theologians, the press and television does not matter anymore and has largely died away. All that early conflict was necessary for me to learn, so that I could reach a higher level of consciousness. I realise that it was all part of my learning and development process. Jesus summed it up very aptly when he said:

'He that wishes to follow me, let him first deny himself and take up his cross daily and follow me.'

What he is effectively saying is that He promises us nothing but a cross to bear, but He also says:

'He that shall endure to the end shall be saved.'

National Federation NSF of Spiritual Healers

BURROWS LEA · SHERE · GUILDFORD · SURREY
PHONE: SHERE 254

HE/DC

6th January, 1961.

Dear Miss Butler,

I am writing to congratulate you upon the successful outcome of your visit to the Cardiff hospital. I have seen the press report and your own personal letter in which it seems to me that you have presented the Federation's views accurately, and your own personal testimonies have been responsible in maintaining the privilege of our members to visit the sick in the Cardiff hospitals.

I this this success is all the more important considering that you had the weight of official medical opinion against you; and the Federation's thanks are yours for your excellent efforts on its behalf.

I shall have much pleasure in bringing your good efforts to the notice of the Council.

With all good wishes.

Yours sincerely,

A letter of congratulation from Harry Edwards.

64

CARDIFF HOSPITAL MANAGEMENT COMMITTEE

Group Secretary :
STANLEY F. BARRY. F.H.A.

Telephone :
Cardiff 29216

YOUR REF.....................

OUR REF. SFB/PH/T9 .

All correspondence to be
addressed to The Group Secretary.

44. CATHEDRAL ROAD,

CARDIFF.

5th January, 1961.

Miss M. Butler,
The Temple of Light,
Glanley Street,
Ystradgynlais,
Nr. Swansea.

Dear Miss Butler,

On behalf of the Chairman and Members of the
Cardiff Hospital Management Committee, I desire to
express to you their grateful thanks for kindly
attending the meeting at St. David's Hospital on
Tuesday, and for so ably putting the Case on behalf
of the National Federation of Spiritual Healers, in
relation to their work at Hospitals.

You will be interested to learn that the
Management Committee by a narrow majority, agreed to
continue the permission granted in my letter to the
Secretary of the National Federation of Spiritual
Healers, dated 2nd March, 1960.

Yours sincerely,

Group Secretary.

A letter of confirmation from the Cardiff Hospital Management Committee.

**Thames
Television**

Thames Television Limited
306-316 Euston Road
London NW1 3BB
01-387 9494 **Ext.** 643

Miss Marian Butler   3rd December, 1975
28 Heol Maes-y-Dre
Ystradgynlais
SWANSEA SA9 1HA

Dear Marian Butler,

    Thank you very much for coming such a long journey to take part in our Faith Healing programme today. I hope you enjoyed the discussion. It all went so very well, and I think you made a very valuable contribution to the subject. I think Professor Taylor was very interested in meeting you, and I hope he will get in touch with you for his researches.

    Transmission will be next Wednesday 10th December at 2 pm but as I mentioned to you, Harlech do not take the programme. Westward Television do transmit it, so if you can manage to get this in your area you will be able to see it. Otherwise, I am afraid it means a journey to the London area. One way or another, I hope you will be able to see the programme, as I think you will enjoy it and consider it well worth while. If I am ever in the Swansea area, I hope to see you and meanwhile, wish you well in your healing work,

            Yours sincerely,

            Valerie Brayden

            Valerie Brayden
            Programme Researcher

A letter from Thames Television.

Chapter Five

DEVELOPING

In the very early days of my development I became involved with the illness of my uncle, Mr. Ivor John Thomas, who was suffering badly from pneumoconiosis. My uncle lived next door to me. At that time he was not able to obtain compensation for the disease, since he had finished work in 1929 and the 'Act' that permitted compensation for those who suffered pneumoconiosis did not come into being until about 1933. I felt strongly that since he had worked most of his life in the pit, compensation was morally justified. As a consequence, I felt compelled to go and meet Mr. Arthur Horner, who was one of the miners' leaders at that time. He was due to give an address to the local mining community at Ystalyfera. After he had given his address to the miners, I went to see him privately. He advised me to go and see Mr. James Evans, who was the local miners' agent, who lived in the neighbouring village of Abercrave. In turn, Mr. Evans contacted the manager of Onllwyn colliery, Mr. John Williams, and asked him if he would interview my uncle with a view to finding him a light job. Personally I did not think that such an interview would take place, since my uncle could only speak a few words without gasping for breath.

Eventually, the colliery manager did agree, to interview him. When I informed my uncle of this good news, he accused me of losing my sanity. Nevertheless, the interview took place on Monday, the following week. It was a very fine day which was ideal for uncle's chest condition, consequently he had little difficulty with his breathing that day. The interview was a success, with the colliery manager giving my uncle a job with light duties underground. My uncle was told to report for work the following week.

He went to the colliery on his first day like a child who had just found a new toy, he was overwhelmed with joy. He signed on for work and was presented with his mining lamp, and entered the pit cage to descend into the mine. The pit cage had just started to descend when my uncle seemed to suffer a heart attack. He was driven home in the colliery car and when he arrived home he looked very ill indeed. He was only home two days when his condition deteriorated even further. When the local doctor visited him, he immediately transferred him to Morriston Hospital, some ten miles away. He was only in hospital about twenty-four hours when he passed away. The doctor in charge of my uncle's case asked my bother, David Ewart Butler, to approach the hospital doctor, Mr. Duncan Davies, for permission from my aunt to carry out a post mortem. This would be necessary in order to ascertain the cause of death. My brother obtained permission to carry out the post mortem. Later that day, I accompanied my brother to visit Mr. Duncan Davies in his office.

Mr. Davies thanked us for obtaining permission for the post mortem. He told us that he could think of four possible reasons for my uncle's death, but did not know the exact cause. As he spoke these words, I found myself falling into a state of suspension. I did not seem to be in full possession of my mind. I seemed to be in a kind of no-man's-land. It was quite a pleasant experience but I could not tell how long it lasted. To me, it seemed to last but for a few seconds only. Just as suddenly I found myself back in full possession of my faculties. To my surprise I sensed a great deal of agitation in the room. Duncan Davies had become angry because of the words which, unbeknown to me, I had just uttered. In my 'suspended' state I had just said, "You must retain the lungs doctor, we want to retain them for full analysis."

Unknown to me then, this was my first experience of the 'trance state'. I had been inspired to use these words by my main Healing Guide, Dr. Clive Osborne. This event took place months before Raheede first spoke through me in my Sanctuary. I realised that there was no way that I could have had the knowledge to utter those words to Mr. Duncan Davies. I later realised that this was proof to me that a Spirit Intelligence had inspired me to use those words. As a consequence of uttering those words, Mr. Davies became very angry and told us to clear out of his office. As we left his office, he informed us that he was putting the whole matter before the local Coroner in Swansea.

After we left, not a single word was spoken between Ewart and I. However, I could see from the look on his face that he was very angry with me. I had once again caused more trouble for him! I tried to explain to Ewart that whatever I had said to Mr. Davies, I had no control over it. My brother told me that he thought that I was mad. The sooner that I gave it all up, the better! Obviously, this was the one thing that I could not do. I could never deny my involvement with the Spirit World.

Later, we caught a bus to Swansea so that we could speak to the Coroner, whose office was located in the police headquarters. During the bus journey, I clearly heard my uncle's voice saying, "He will not be there." So I turned to my brother and said to him, "The Coroner will not be there." And he replied, "Now I know you are mad! It's because of you we have to go and see him in the first place."

When we arrived, we were shown into the Coroner's office by a police sergeant, who turned to us and said, "I am very sorry the Coroner is not here. He has been called away urgently to attend a suicide case." My brother turned to look at me, but did not say a word. The state of cold war still remained between us. Before we left, I explained to the sergeant why we were there in the first place. He turned to me and stated that the Coroner still wanted to see us. "You have really put your foot in it this time," said the sergeant. "By challenging the establishment, you really have put the cat amongst the pigeons." The sergeant however, did seem to have some sympathy for us. He informed us that the post mortem was presently in progress and that he had been instructed to send my uncle's lungs to the pathologist, Dr. Sladden. As we were about to leave I said to the sergeant, "That was the best bit of news that I have heard all week." As we left the office the sergeant further informed us that we should report to the Coroner's office again on the following Saturday.

On the following Saturday, my brother and I were once again on the bus to Swansea. After sitting for about ten minutes, I heard my uncle's voice saying to me once again, "He won't be there."

I conveyed this information to my brother, who turned to me and said, "You said that last Thursday."

"Was I right or was I wrong?" I replied.

"You are just assuming that the same thing is going to happen again today," said Ewart.

As we approached the Coroner's office, the sergeant opened the door very sheepishly for us.

"He has been called away again, he is with some government officers this time," said the sergeant. "However, he has decided to release the body for burial. You had better ring the undertaker as soon as possible."

Ewart immediately telephoned the undertaker from the Coroner's office. Then the sergeant accompanied us to the Registrar's office so that we could collect the death certificate. I was asked to wait outside. And as they entered the Office, I overheard the sergeant as he turned to my brother and said, "She is a queer one isn't she? She has not put a foot wrong." The primary cause of death was due to chronic venus congestion, caused by chronic bronchitis, emphysema and *pneumoconiosis*!

The fact that my uncle had been employed in the mining industry for a second time, although it was very briefly, entitled his widow to claim full compensation. This however, was not the end of the matter. When we arrived home that Saturday afternoon, I felt very elated that justice at last had been done. After all my uncle had worked most of his working life down the pit. Nevertheless, I had the distinct impression that somehow or other, other people were involved with this case. The police sergeant had already informed us that the lungs had been sent to an independent panel of doctors for assessment. Dr. Sladden had said that my uncle's lungs were in one of the worst conditions that he had ever seen. Only about one and a quarter lungs were functioning. We therefore had to await the final verdict by the independent panel of doctors in Sheffield.

Just after my uncle's death, on the 18th May, 1951, my niece and I went to Porthcawl for a week's holiday. We could only afford to stay in a small guest house, therefore during the day we had to leave our accommodation. As it rained almost every day, we were forced to spend a lot of our time drinking tea and coffee in various cafes. One day, I suggested it would be a good idea to go to the cinema for a change.

When we arrived at the cinema, we noticed that it was only open in the evening. On reading the notice-board outside the cinema, we noticed that there was a Spiritualist Service in the cinema that afternoon, so we went. When the service ended, it was announced that there would be another in the local Spiritualist Church later in the evening, but when we arrived at the church, we had to queue outside in the pouring rain for about forty-five minutes. When we eventually got in, the service began with a Clairvoyant Demonstration by a lady from Leicester. I was the first person she spoke to when she turned to me to say, "I have a gentleman here, he says his name is Ivor." She spoke these words with a distressed breathing state.

"He says his name is Ivor John Thomas, and says he has a message for Marian. Who is Marian?" asked the medium.

"Me," I replied.

"Who is Elizabeth?" she asked.

"It's my aunt," I replied.

"Ivor says that he has come back to you to thank you for what you did for him with Mr. Duncan Davies, at Morriston Hospital.

I realised the complete authenticity of these statements, which totally convinced me of Spirit Life. This event was to set the seal on my own mediumship. The medium concluded her conversation with me by saying that we would be notified in the last week of October and that compensation would be granted in the last week of November. That is exactly what happened. That experience was one that I well never, never forget.

I remember one summer evening being called to the bedside of an elderly lady who had a massive cancerous growth in her throat. She could not eat or swallow and was gradually getting weaker and weaker. The end of her life was nearing. The only moisture that could enter her body was by way of small drops of water, placed on her lips, which she could slowly lick on her tongue. Whilst I was praying and giving her the 'Laying on of Hands', I thought to myself, "If there was only something that I could do for her to ease her pain." Eventually, I had to leave her and journey home again. And as I was walking home, I looked up to the clear skies of the Heavenworld and wondered what I could do to help her. Suddenly the words of the Great Master Healer, Jesus Christ, came into my mind: 'Marvel not at the things that I do, greater things than this ye shall do, because I go unto my father.'

Suddenly it came into my mind: "If I could only get some water into her body!" Then, I remembered the miracle of Jesus, where He turned the water into wine at the wedding feast at Cana, Galilee. What was there to prevent me from asking God to convert water into medicine which could be used as a curative force? I had nothing to lose, but everything to gain. I decided when I reached home I would turn my thoughts into reality. I immediately took an empty bottle from the cupboard, washed it clean and filled it with fresh tap-water. I took the bottle into the Sanctuary of the front room of my home. In prayer, I asked God to convert the water into healing medicine. At the same time I made the needs of the poor lady known to him.

When I went to visit the lady again the next day, I took the bottle of water with me. I told the people who were looking after her that rather than use ordinary tap-water to moisten her lips, they should use the water that I had brought with me. I told them that it was 'blessed water'. Slowly but surely, a miracle happened. As they placed the water on her lips, more and more often she made signs that she wanted another drink. The water was placed on her lips with the tip of a teaspoon. Gradually, this developed into a quarter of a teaspoon, then into half a teaspoon and then into a full teaspoon. Slowly, this progressed into a dessertspoonful and then a tablespoonful. Eventually, she was able to swallow a wine glass full of water. From then on she progressed to a good state of health. During the latter part of her life she told me that she continued to thank God in her normal place of worship. She eventually died at a very old age of senility, but without a trace of cancer in her body.

This experience naturally opened up a tremendous avenue of thought in my mind. As I continued through life, I thought that I would use the 'blessed water' again and again. I did this very often. As patients came to me for healing I would ask them, "Are you prepared to try an experiment?" I almost always told them that it was an experiment. I also told them that I could not guarantee that the water would work. But it did work, time and time again it worked. I witnessed the use of the water clearing skin rashes. I have seen it used successfully to clear warts. I saw it heal many various conditions. Today, the use of 'blessed water' has become very much part of my life. I have used it now for more than twenty years and still use it almost every day of my life. I have imparted this knowledge to all my colleagues who work with me in the Healing field. They too have become part of this Divine manifestation. Did God not create the water in the first place? Did it not also become effective at Cana, Galilee? I ask you to believe me for I know that the answer is most positively, yes.

Although most of my life has been spent amongst sickness and melancholy, nevertheless my life has had many humorous moments. I can for example recall one particular incident which occurred during one of our regular 'sittings' whilst I was in the trance state. At that time, I was developing physical powers, and physical phenomena was very relevant in my life. It was on a Saturday evening when the last sitter entered my room to confirm that she had locked the door. However, as it turned out, she could not have checked it thoroughly enough. In fact the door had been left unlocked, making it possible for anybody to walk into the room, and that is precisely what happened.

I was in the 'trance state' and Raheede my Guide was speaking, when suddenly, four drunken men, who must have heard us talking, pushed the door open and entered into the room in which we were sitting. As they entered the room, my co-sitters were naturally very apprehensive. However, my Guide 'Raheede' spoke to these men and said to them, "Welcome, my brothers."

On hearing his words, they had such a fright that they all darted out of the room as fast as their legs could carry them. They were falling over themselves in the stampede. That was the last that we ever saw of them.

During other phases of my mediumship, I worked with a man in the Spirit World who was a tremendous scientist. His name was Sir Oliver Lodge. Many people had sworn to me that they had seen his face above the cabinet in which I was sitting. (At that time, I used to sit in a closed cabinet. The cabinet being essential for physical mediumship, so that the power can be condensed into a small space.) I was told that Sir Oliver used to appear quite regularly at that period. During his presence, I used to sense a kind of aura around me which was completely different to anything else that I had experienced. The first thing that I noticed was that my lips had become completely sealed. This would invariably happen at the start of the sitting, just after we had sung the *Lord's Prayer*. As soon as we had finished singing, my lips became so tight that it seemed as if they had been physically screwed together. Even the act of moistening my own lips was impossible. I did not like this experience at all, for it seemed as if someone was tampering with my physical body. It was later explained to me by other researchers of physical mediumship that most mediums had had similar experiences. However, it must be remembered that I had no knowledge what was happening to me for I had no tutoring or guidance from anyone in the physical world and everything that happened to me was all strange territory to me.

At a later stage, I felt that there was something building up at the side of my throat. Of course, I did not know what was happening, consequently I would often ask the leader of our circle to ask the Guide what was happening to my physical body. The Guide explained that the Spirit World was building up an independent 'voice-box', which could be used for direct voice communication from the Spirit World. Sometimes, perhaps on two or three occasions, the 'direct voice' spoke. However, on most occasions, communication was mostly in the 'independent voice', when the Spirit would speak through my voice.

When the direct voice communication occurred I began to feel much stronger in my physical body, but the tightness in my lips still persisted. I later discovered from my Guide why my lips were sealed. He said they had been sealed so as to prevent me from interfering in any way with the ectoplasm that would emanate from my mouth. Eventually ectoplasm did commence, it started by emanating from my mouth and then from my waist. From the waist, the ectoplasm was in the form of a fine mist. As it emanated from my mouth it took a form which was more like syrup in texture. This syrup became very thick and white in appearance. From my sitting position, the ectoplasm would broaden out to about six to eight inches in width and would reach all the way down to the floor.

My 'sitters' later informed me, that within the ectoplasm that had emanated from my mouth, they could often see the faces of animals, humans, and other objects. These events continued for a very considerable period of time, however, an apport never materialised.

Later, I began to feel other strange occurrences happening to my body. It was explained to us, through my Guide, that there were two Guides in the Spirit World who wanted to use me as their medium. One group of Guides wanted to use me purely for the development of physical phenomena and wanted me to discontinue with my healing work. The other group of Guides wanted to use me purely for Spiritual Healing. I was never forced into a decision, they told me that I had my own free will.

Naturally I felt that I too needed guidance, consequently, I journeyed with Gwenda to London and managed to have a sitting with Horrace Leaf, who at that time was a famous physical medium. He was a powerful medium, and was capable of both materialisation and direct voice communication. During the sitting his Guide informed me that this effective duel was going on because both groups of Guides wanted to use me for different phenomena. Eventually, I decided that if Spirit wanted to use me for physical phenomena then I would follow their wishes. As a consequence, for a period of two to three weeks, I stopped any form of healing work. Healing was still going on in my Sanctuary, but this was being carried out by my colleagues Ossie West and Gwenda Jones.

After I had reached my decision, (it was unknown to me, although I was later informed about it) there was still a considerable amount of debate in the Spirit World about my decision. One day, Ossie West became ill and was unable to carry on the healing work, Gwenda also became ill at this time. This meant that there was no one to carry on with the healing work. However, those patients who were very sick, still needed healing. This filled me with compassion for their needs. I therefore asked God for some grace so that I could carry on with the healing work until such time as my colleagues were well again. I could then return to my work with physical phenomena. However, all sorts of snags and hindrances seemed to be put in my way, which prevented me from returning to my physical mediumship. I then realised what was happening, it was the Healing Guides who wanted to use me. In prayer I decided that I would serve the world of Spirit to the very best of my ability and that I would devote myself to healing and discontinue with physical phenomena. This decision was much to the disappointment of my sitters. Nevertheless, I have always retained my gift of trance mediumship and I am certain that this gift will always remain with me until the day I leave my earthly body.

I have found the trance state such an invaluable asset, because it has enabled me to do so much more work in helping others; helping the bereaved; helping people who are in desperate financial situations; to heal broken marriages; helping to find children who have absconded from their homes. Without the trance state I would never have had the ability, understanding or insight of knowing how to tackle such diverse problems. All this has been made possible through my beloved Guide, Raheede, who was able to utilise the knowledge of those on the other side of life, in the Spirit World, to bring about a reconciliation for the different types of problems that people have. Even to this day, I find myself being hurled more and more into the area of true love and compassion. I thank God every day that I am able to help people overcome the many obstacles of life.

From the first time that I became a Channel for Raheede, he was able to open our minds so that we could understand what was happening and how the healing energies were being released. He prophesied that people would come from the North, South, East, and West. Ewart, who was sitting with us, questioned Raheede and asked him, "Who is going to tell them?" How are they going to be brought here?"

"Don't worry, my Brother," said Raheede, "they will draw to the light like moths draw to the lamp."

Indeed, this statement, has been proven to be correct, many, many times during my mediumship.

We carried on with the development of my mediumship in this manner for two solid years. One day a request was made to me: "Would you become instrumental in healing a child patient?" But one of my 'sitters' said that this would not be possible, since she felt that no child should be brought into a seance room. However, I felt very strongly that if a child was sick, we could give healing at the start of our sitting. The child, after having healing, could then leave the room, allowing us to carry on with our development work in the circle. That is what eventually transpired. However, we did not seem to be achieving very much. We never had any spectacular occurances.

Events led me to feel very compassionate towards my young niece, Margaret. Since a little child, Margaret had suffered terribly from psoriasis, and her little body was very unsightly. Psoriasis covered her arms and legs and was very troublesome to her. One day, I decided that I would take her on holiday with me to London. Once there I took her to visit the headquarters of the Spiritualist Association of Great Britain (S.A.G.B.) so that we could visit Nan McKenzie, who was a 'trance medium' who had an Indian Guide by the name of Running Water. We then made an appointment for Margaret and me to meet her. When we arrived at the S.A.G.B., we were shown into a little Healing room. At that time Margaret was about nine years old, she was taking violin lessons. Whilst Running Water was giving Margaret her healing treatment, he said to her, "Place your arms out, my sister. These are the arms that give out such wonderful vibrations as you play the violin." I was very thrilled to hear these words, since I had not mentioned to anyone that Margaret could play any musical instrument to anyone. From then on everything seemed such a reality to me.

We left the S.A.G.B. headquarters and returned to our abode in London and then home to Wales. As time went by, I noticed that Margaret, who instead of getting better, was getting progressively, very much worse. She seemed to be continuously deteriorating. However, Running Water had told me this would occur before she would get better. He said that two years from the day that he had given her healing, she would be clear, free of all the psoriasis, and I say to all those who may read this book, that is exactly what did happen. Running Water had predicted that it would take two years to cure her, and that is exactly how long it took, two years to the day. There was not a mark left on her body. She has savoured that wonderful experience ever since.

After that wonderful experience, our circle progressed, until the day arrived when we were challenged to treat a man with a tumour who worked in the local clock factory. At that time, he endured terrific pain and had been treated for this condition by a number of hospitals in both England and Wales. When I gathered with my circle of friends, we agreed to see him and establish if we could do anything to help. After speaking to him for some time, I suggested that he could take part in an experiment. I said we would try to see if Spirit could help directly rather than me treat him indirectly. It was suggested by Raheede that he would invite Ebernazin to come along to see what he could do to help this man's condition. During that particular evening, my dear friend in Spirit, Ebernazin, who was a surgeon, came to us. Ebernazin asked for the assistance of my brother Ewart and Elizabeth Anne Jones, who was an elderly member of our circle. Both these assisted in carrying out a psychic operation on this man's brain, under the direction of Ebernazin.

About two weeks after this man had had his psychic operation, he went to hospital for his routine check-up. To his wonderment, he was informed that he did not have a tumour any more. The doctors told him that for some unknown reason, the tumour had either dispersed or they had made an incorrect diagnosis in the first place. Nevertheless, he continued a normal life for many, many years after and became a regular member of the church services that took place every Sunday evening.

Another patient that comes to mind around this period was Mrs. Davies. This lady was blind, and I think she suffered from a detached retina. After a few visits to my Sanctuary, I became aware of something that was sticking into my fingers. I did not know what it was, but it felt very sharp. I asked myself, "What could this be?" but I never came up with an answer. You must remember that this event took place very early on in my healing ministry. I had not had sufficient experience to establish what it was all about.

A few weeks later, Mrs. Davies was lying in bed adjacent to the bedroom window in her home, eating her breakfast, when she suddenly shouted out aloud that she could actually see the people that she had recognised from years previously. When members of her family rushed upstairs to see what was wrong, she said that she could see! A few days later a couple of pieces of metal appeared high on her cheek. When she touched them, she was able to wipe them away easily and without pain. She showed these pieces to her doctor so that he could confirm what they were. Happily, she was able to see quite clearly for many years to come until she finally passed away.

Another extraordinary incident happened around Easter time, when beloved Aunt Bess's best friend, Marie Price, passed on into the Higher Life. As a consequence, Aunt Bess wanted some very special flowers to be placed in the Sanctuary as a mark of respect for her friend. At this time, my aunt and her best friend used to sing duets together almost every Sunday evening without fail. It was always a joy and a pleasure for us to listen to them.

When I asked her what type of flowers I should get, "Oh get whatever you think best," replied Aunt Bess. So, on the Saturday, I went to the local flower nursery, and my eyes caught sight of some beautiful white tulips and also some deep purple irises. At the same time, I felt that there was some significance to these colours, yet I could not fully understand what it was. Later, I went up to my aunt's friend's house to offer my condolences to her family. I told them that we would hold a memorial service for her in our Sanctuary, the next day, which was Sunday. I told the family that we had bought flowers and that we had chosen white tulips and the deepest of blue irises that were available. The family informed me that those were her favourite blend of flowers. It became obvious that we had been guided to select them.

On the following day, the Memorial Service took place as planned. During the service, I was standing quite close to the flowers. As the invocation was being given, I suddenly heard an unusual rustling sound, which forced me to open my eyes so that I could see what was happening. Before my eyes, I could see the flowers moving around the Sanctuary and at the same time being rearranged. Then everyone else in the room became aware of what was happening. At this point, we suspended the invocation. The flowers rose out of the original vase and proceeded to another, in full view of the thirty people who were in the house. We all witnessed the white tulips and the blue irises separating; whereas previously mixed together, they now had become separated in different vases. Just as suddenly, we all witnessed the blue irises turn white and the white tulips turn blue. This was a source of great amazement to all of us. That experience will be another one that I shall treasure for the rest of my life. A little later, everything became very quiet, with hardly a sound to be heard. In this silence I became aware and thankful for what I had just witnessed. I continued with the invocation and the flowers remained unchanged. After I had given the Benediction, we began to close the service with a hymn. At the same time, we all began to hear a rustling sound again. As we looked around, we could all see that the flowers were on the move again. The tulips and the irises returned to their original positions, mixed together in the manner that we had arranged them initially.

To anyone who has not witnessed such an event, I can imagine that it would be a source of amusement and laughter. However, I swear that this event was absolutely authentic. I hold that experience as a very sacred event which I will treasure for as long as I live, and I am sure that this applies to all the people who were present that day.

Another important event in my life also remains very vivid in my mind. In this case, it relates to absent or distant healing, which was indeed a very unusual experience. It all started by contact with Michelangelo, during the period when I was doing healing work in Burgstadtenfells, Germany. On this particular day, we had made a visit to Liechtenstein and by chance we were in a restaurant inside one of the many castles. All the members of our group were seated around one table. Out of the corner of my eye, I noticed a young man, who was probably in his late twenties. He noticed me too and smiled at me. In return I also smiled and nodded my head. I asked him if he could speak English. "Nein," he replied. I then tried to explain to him that I could not speak German. Finally I raised my hands as if to explain that alas there was nothing we could do about the situation.

A little later, a lady approached me and I naturally asked her if she could speak English. "Yes, very well," she replied. She continued by explaining to me that she had been a teacher. In turn, I explained to her that I would like to make contact with the young German who could not speak English.

"Can you help me please," I asked. "I have a message for him but unfortunately I cannot speak German and he cannot speak English."

"He is a friend of my husband, his name is Herr Untersee," replied the lady.

The young man was invited to come and sit next to me at the end of the table, just long enough for me to give him the message that I had received from Spirit. Through my interpreter I asked the young man, "Are you an artist?"

"Ja," he replied.

"I understand that you have an exhibition and that you are worried about it."

My lady friend translated this to him.

"Ja," he once again replied.

I informed him that I had seen a gentleman standing next to him and that my Guide had said that his name was Michelangelo. I also informed him that he was having difficulty in formulating the correct blue colour which he had been long searching for in his paintings. He just could not obtain the correct shade of blue. I could see from the look on his face that he was quite amazed by these statements. After further translation, he once again replied, "Ja."

"Michelangelo is going to help you," I continued.

Later in the evening, after we had finished our meal, he invited me to his studio. In fact we were all invited to see his work. He seemed particularly pleased that I had accompanied him, for he had just received a very important message. As we walked through the studio, the interpreter informed me that Herr Untersee would like to progress with his own psychic work. In addition he promised me that if my messages turned out to be true, and that if his exhibition was able to proceed, he would present me with an album of his works.

After the healing tour had ended, I returned home to Wales. One day, I received an unexpected parcel through the door. When I opened it, I could see that it was an album of Herr Untersee's paintings. The small album contained photographs of his most recent works, most of which had been painted in the most beautiful shades of blue imaginable. I still treasure that album today since it brings me fond memories of that period in my life.

Later, Herr Untersee wrote me a letter from Liechtenstein, or rather he drew me a letter. Since he was a good artist and he could not speak English nor could I speak German, the letter which I received contained a series of sketches depicting the health condition of his mother. Through deep thought I was able to understand what he was trying to express. One of the sketches showed his mother lying on her bed, unable to move, above her head, there was a boxed arrow saying, "Help." Another sketch depicted me standing over her with my hands emitting energy in the form of light rays. Consequently, in thought, I started to work upon his mother and I sensed that she was a little better. I also began to realise that in some way, her illness was connected with fear; fear associated with the past War, and fear for the safety of her family who had lived in Germany. As I continued to work mentally on her condition, I was unable to find out the exact cause. However, I realised that the Healing Guides would be able to deal with the situation and would be able to direct the appropriate healing.

The next letter I received from Herr Untersee was again in sketch-form. In this case, however, the sketches showed his mother in bed, but this time sitting in an upright position. Whereas previously she could not hold anything in her hands, this time, she was holding a cup of coffee. Later sketches showed her sitting up in bed, but with one leg out of bed touching the floor. Subsequent sketches showed her with both legs on the floor. Later she was depicted as being able to stand, holding the top of the bed for support. This progressed to the stage where she was able to walk about in her home. Finally, she was shown sitting out in her garden enjoying the sunshine. The last sketch also had written on it, the word "Danke", thank you.

This experience was a particular joy to me for it proved that a healing could take place without the need of written communication other than the sort of communication that took place in the sketches.

IO 709094

(Printed by authority of the Registrar-General)

D. Cert.
R.B.D.

The Statutory Fee for this Certificate is 3s. 6d. together with 1d. Stamp Duty. Where a search is necessary to find the entry, a Search Fee is payable in addition.

CERTIFIED COPY of an ENTRY OF DEATH.

Pursuant to the Births and Deaths Registration Acts, 1836 to 1947.

Insert in this Margin any Notes which appear in the original entry.

Registration District SWANSEA

1951. Death in the Sub-district of .... in the ....

No.	When and where Died.	Name and Surname.	Sex.	Age.	Rank or Profession.	Cause of Death.	Signature, Description and Residence of Informant.	When Registered.	Signature of Registrar.
Columns:—	1	2	3	4	5	6	7	8	9
49.	Tenth May 1951 Morriston Emergency Hospital U.D.	Ivor John Thomas	Male	62 Years	J Stanley Stuart Ystradgynlais R.D. Retired (underground)	Pneumoconiosis congestion due to chronic bronchitis emphysema + pneumoconiosis. Acute retention of urine due to hypertrophy of the middle lobe of the prostate gland, certified by Bond & Clarke. "Post Mortem without inquest.	J.S. Butler 21 Oldest Ystradgynlais Swansea	Twelfth May 1951	M Haynes Deputy
									Registrar.

I, M Haynes Deputy, Registrar of Births and Deaths for the Sub-District of Swansea, in the County Borough, in the Register Book of Deaths for the said Sub-District, and that such Register Book is now legally in my custody, do hereby certify that this is a true copy of the Entry No. 49.

WITNESS MY HAND this 18th day of May, 1951.

M Haynes Deputy, Registrar of Births and Deaths.

CAUTION.—Any person who (1) falsifies any of the particulars on this Certificate, or (2) uses it as true, knowing it to be falsified, is liable to Prosecution.

1d. Stamp to be affixed and cancelled

Uncle Ivor's Death Certificate, confirming his death was from pneumoconiosis.

82

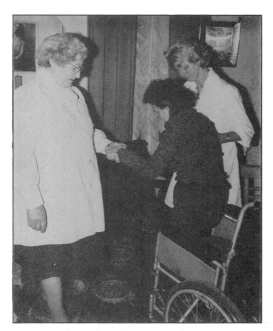

A typical Healing Session at the Sanctuary.

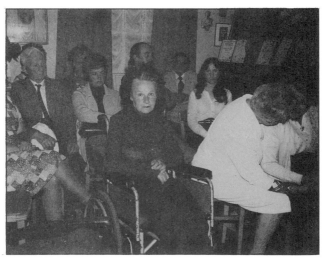

At home . . . 28, Heol Maes y Dre, Ystdradgynlais.

Marian Butler during Spiritual Healing.

A German Shepherd Dog receives Spiritual Healing.

Chapter Six

CONCENTRATION CAMPS

One year I was invited to Salzburg, Austria, to take a seminar and also demonstrate the power of Spiritual Healing. Coinciding with my stay there was the Mozart festival, which is held in January every year. My hosts had presented me with a book of tickets that would enable me to visit any concert, be it string quartet, symphony orchestra, violin, piano, or flute concerto, and one day, when I was going to listen to a piano concerto being played by the Vienna Philharmonic Orchestra, I reflected back to the period when the Mozartium was a great light in the world. It gave so much pleasure and happiness to many, many people.

I had also been invited to a place called Mauthausen. This name or place did not mean anything to me at the time. I might have heard it mentioned, but it never registered in my mind. My hostess, Dr. Marian Mentel, who was an historian who lived in Salzburg, advised me not to go near the place. She said that I was too sensitive a person. So I asked her, "What is it about the place?"

"It is a museum now, she said, but previously it was a concentration camp."

Eventually, it was agreed that Dr. Marian Mentel, Anne Marie Fuchs Lechner and I would go there.

I can't say that I relished going there, but it had always been a policy in my life, that when I made a promise, I tried to keep it, at least to the very best of my ability. So I went to Mauthausen, and I can still vividly recall my feelings of that day when I walked into hell. I had never experienced such feelings before in my life. I think that every vent in my body was opened to all the kinds of suffering that mankind had experienced in every hut in that camp. It really was beyond man's understanding.

When one walks through the gates of Mauthausen, one can feel the aura of desolation, of degradation and the humiliation of the poor souls that had suffered there. When I walked through Mauthausen I experienced many horrific impressions. When I entered the last section of the camp I felt as if something or someone was trying to combine with my soul. I could not explain these feelings or put a finger on it at that time. However, they were the most horrific feelings that I have ever experienced. The sensations were those of ugliness and revenge. Yet all that I was giving out was love, compassion, understanding, and mercy. There was a kind of duel going on all the time in my mind. I remained in Austria for another two weeks after my visit to Mauthausen, yet those feelings never left me. Then one night, as I was travelling back to Ostend in Belgium, from Austria, I realised that those experiences that I had had in Mauthausen were but another form of Spiritual Healing. Those poor souls who had died there in all that misery, had to face another misery, that of awaking out of the 'Death Sleep'.

The 'Death Sleep' was something that I had never heard of before. I obtained such information about the 'Death Sleep' from the Guides. They explained that a poor soul was awakening out of the 'Death Sleep' at the very time that I was walking through Mauthausen. It occurred to me when I was near to the crematorium, where the bodies were put into the ovens. A poor female soul had been there for a great number of years. During all that time, she relived in the memory closet of her mind, all the suffering that she had endured. She did not realise that she was awakening into a brand new world. However, as her mind began to become activated, she began to realise that she was residing in a different dimension, but this situation had left her in a confused state. This new dimension was only in the form of a picture, as yet, it had not become a reality to her.

At that time, I was wearing thick, high leather boots, and I soon realised that she was unable to see me from the waist upwards, for she had been forced to sit on the floor with her arms above her head, chained to the wall. She had been waiting her turn to be taken to the ovens to be cremated. I could see from the position of her legs that she had been kept in a sitting position. During this mental communication, I too was awakened to the true reality of Spiritual Healing. Although she was making her first steps into the Spiritual World, her mind was still functioning on the Earth Plane. She must have thought that I was one of the wardresses who had brutally tortured her and she was hell-bent on getting revenge. However, because of my involvement with those wonderful Guides on the other side who were now using me as a healing channel, she was not able to penetrate my aura. The Guides were now protecting me and that was a reality.

In the last section of the camp, people had been held prisoner, chained to the walls, sitting on the floor. Later, they were dragged out to have any gold removed from their teeth, then laid on stretchers ready to be placed alive into the ovens. These experiences I will never, ever forget on this side of my life. I know with certainty that when my life is ended, I will meet up with those poor souls I first met on that day.

When I looked at my hostess friend who had taken me to that place, I said to her, "I don't know about you, but I am ready to leave."

"Me too," she replied as we both walked out of the room.

Since I could see that my friend was upset, I put my arm around her waist and said to her, "Let us both find God, since we are both very fortunate to be able to walk out of the camp, unlike the thousands who had been imprisoned here."

At that time, that seemed to be the end of the matter, but it was not to be. It was only the beginning of another chapter of my understanding of spiritual life. When we finally arrived back in Salzburg, we washed, changed and had something to eat. Later, I was taken to the Mozartium, where I listened to the most wonderful creative music of Mozart. I gazed at the rostrum, watching the geniuses at work. They truly were geniuses, since they had to train for many, many years before they were even accepted into the Vienna School of Music. They then had to attend that School of Music for ten years before they were allowed to perform with the orchestra in public. As I sat there listening to the wonderful renderings of Mozart's music, my mind also thought of that dreadful camp that we had visited earlier in the day. Sitting on one side of me was a German lady, on the other, a Dutch lady. The music was truly wonderful. Can you imagine the strings of the *Ave Verum* competing against the wailings, mournings, sufferings and tortuous screams of those poor people at the concentration camp?

As I sat there reflecting upon the life that we had experienced during the war years, the German and Dutch ladies turned to look at me and I turned to look at them. However, it was apparent to me that they were not thinking what I was thinking. As I looked at the orchestra, I suddenly had a terrible vision, it was as if a black tar-like substance was seeping down from the midst of that concentration camp and overflowing into the middle of the orchestra. Just as suddenly, a pure gold colour appeared, seeming to change the black tar-like substance into a lighter and lighter colour until it turned into silver. A beautiful light then began to turn and go upwards, as if in a crescendo of colour, up through the ceiling. That was also an experience which I shall never forget. I thought that too would be the end of the experience.

After the performance ended, my hostess and I returned to Salzburg. By this time, she had become very concerned about me and said that I would not be able to sleep alone after experiencing such horrors. True, I was unable to sleep for a while because my mind continued to think of those poor souls at the camp. Nevertheless, I could sense my friend Raheede, so supportive in every way, was close to me. He told me not to be fearful, and that the experience was part of my healing work.

On my journey home from Austria, I realised that the female soul was accompanying me. As I arrived home and opened the front door to the Sanctuary in my aunt's house, that poor soul entered into the most brilliant spiritual light that she had ever experienced. What an awakening for her! Although she had aligned her mind with mine so that she could obtain revenge, in the end, she found light and compassion at the very end of a very long, dark tunnel.

Of course that was not to be the end of the story. After that imprisoned soul had experienced the awakening, she came in contact with one of my Healing Guides, Dr. Karl Hoffman, who was an Austrian. He took her under his spiritual wing, educated her and released her soul from the terrible suffering. She had two choices to make. Firstly, she could be released into the realms of Spirit, free to explore and to be reunited with her loved ones. Alternatively, she could become a servant of God and act as a helper or mentor to return to the numerous concentration camps such as Auchschwitz, Triblinka, Mauthausen, Dachau, Ravensbruck, Belsen, Buchenwald and many others to await and help the other poor souls who would eventually awaken out of the 'Death Sleep'. It was the latter choice which she decided to take. To this day, she has been acting as a Guide, one of the many Guides who work with Raheede, rescuing those souls who awaken out of the 'Death Sleep' and taking them on their way. She has since rescued about twenty-four thousand other poor souls who have come out of the 'Death Sleep'. They too, have their decisions to make, but she is able to help them along whichever path they choose.

This too is another form of Spiritual Healing!

After the very powerful effect on me which the visit to the concentration camp at Mauthausen had made, it was but a few years later when I returned to Austria again. I once again visited Salzburg, a city which I have since visited on numerous occasions. This time, my friend Ceilia and I were on holiday together. I remember going to bed one Sunday evening, it was pouring with rain and the wind was blowing gale-force. It was about 11 p.m. when we eventually retired to bed. I had no inclination to read, so I decided that I would immediately go to sleep. Conversely, my friend Ceilia who was in her own bed at the opposite corner of the room to me, decided that she would read for a short while. It was not long before I fell asleep. At about 4.20 a.m. I awoke suddenly to find myself screaming the room down. My friend Ceilia rushed over to my bed and wondered what on earth was going on. She enquired if I was sick. I told her that I had had a most vivid nightmare.

"Do you want to talk about it?" she asked.

I explained to her all about the nightmare that I had just experienced. (Of course, today, I realise that it was not a nightmare, it was a visitation from the Spirit World.) I explained to her that I was one of four women travelling in a car and we were going on a very long journey. After about two hours, we decided to stop at a garage and fill up with petrol. As we got out of the car, it occurred to me that it was the most wonderful garage that I had ever seen in my whole life. There were flowers in abundance all around the forecourt. I remembered that the roses were particularly beautiful. I wondered to myself how such beautiful flowers could bloom so well amongst all the petrol fumes that surrounded the garage. I eventually got back into the car, and after continuing on our journey, we had perhaps only driven for a couple of miles, we turned into one of the largest car parks that I had ever seen. It contained an abundance of vehicles of every description, including motor cars, vans, coaches, bicycles, motor-bicycles and mopeds, etc., together with numerous people, some of whom were hikers. When we stopped, I got out of the car and heard my, 'Sisters' calling me. I have never had a sister, I only had two brothers. However, I definitely heard my 'Sisters' calling me. They wanted me to come to them so that they could show me something. I left my three female friends in the car and I proceeded in the direction from which I had heard my 'Sisters'' voices. I never actually saw the 'Sisters', I only heard their voices. When I arrived at the point from which the voices were emanating, I still could not actually see anyone but the 'voices' said to me, "Look Marian, look and see."

I soon realised that I was looking at a large lake of blood, bright red in colour. Feeding the lake was a large-diameter pipe. This flowed with blood, which was a deep crimson in colour. The horror of this scene together with the emanations which it portrayed, frightened me. It was these horrific scenes that had caused me to scream and awaken out of my sleep. After I had shared this experience with my friend, I eventually went back to sleep. When morning eventually came around, I awoke at about 8 a.m. and we prepared as normal for breakfast.

As we entered the breakfast room, we heard people discussing the screams that they had heard in the night. To cover my embarrassment, we both said that we too had heard the screams, but did not know where they had come from. After breakfast, my two other friends from Salzburg collected us by car. They explained that they were unable to take us to Innsbruck as had been initially planned. They said that there was dense fog on the mountain, which would prevent us from seeing anything. They suggested that they would take us on an alternative journey, to where, I did not know. I never questioned them, we just entered the car and drove off.

We had been driving for about two hours, when we had to stop for petrol. As we entered the garage forecourt, I began to recognise the surroundings, which seemed familiar to me, although I knew that I had not been there before. After we had filled the tank with petrol, we all got back into the car and continued on our journey for about another two miles. We turned left and entered a huge car park. It was exactly the same car park that I had seen in my nightmare the previous night. I told my friend Ceilia that this was the place that I had seen in my nightmare. However, I did not breathe a word about it to any of my other friends who were with us in the car. I soon realised that I was going to some horrific place. As I got out of the car, everything that I saw was exactly as I had seen in my nightmare; the cars, vans, mopeds, etc., were all there before my eyes. I wondered deep in my heart, where we were going. We entered some gates, but I did not know exactly were we were.

To my left I noticed a shop which sold candles, rosary beads, crucifixes, bibles, and many kinds of religious gifts. My friends went to the ladies' toilets and I was left alone by the shop. As I entered the shop, at first there was no one there to serve me, but I could hear the patter of feet at the rear of the shop. A lady appeared, and to my surprise, she was a nun, a sister of mercy. Suddenly I gave out the cry, "Oh my God!"

She rebuked me by saying that I should not use the Lord's name in vain.

"I did not do that," I replied, and I told her that I had said it in a state of shock.

"I have just realised where I am, or at least I think I know where I am."

"Don't you know," said the Sister. "You are in Dachau Concentration Camp!"

It was only now that I fully realised what I was being exposed to. What I had experienced was not a nightmare, it was a reality! Knowledge had entered my mind, which was generating information. I realised that what I had experienced was not a nightmare after all, but a visitation from Spirit. When I described the gist of my nightmare to the Sister, she told me, "That was a visitation from God." She also recounted to me a story that had happened recently in the camp.

"It was about seven weeks ago, that I and another sister entered the camp crematorium. There we saw the largest ant-hill that we had ever seen in our lives. The ants were very active carrying small pieces of earth and grit. We were very suspicious of what was inside the ant-hill."

In concentration camps it is normal practice to employ workers, who are paid by the Austrian or German governments, who on finding any human remains at the camps, ensure that these are given a proper burial service and placed in consecrated ground. This was normally carried out after a pathologist had first performed a post mortem, so that it could be established which part of the anatomy the remains belonged to.

The Sister continued by saying that they returned to the convent and reported the large ant-hill that they had seen the previous day, to the camp foreman. He in turn investigated the site. She also informed me that under the ant-hill they found a large-diameter pipe, which extended several metres into the earth. Later, it was established that the pipe contained numerous bones of young Jewish boys, all under the age of seven years. For the rest of my stay, I was exposed to the horrors that had taken place at the camp and I became separated from the rest of my friends. There were many thousands of people visiting the camp that day, so I was not alone. In fact I spoke to many of the visitors, in particular, I remember speaking to a teacher and his wife who came from Denmark. I did not know their names, for I did not ask. However, I discovered that he was a teacher of English. The teacher asked, "Did this really happen madam? You are of an age to remember if such events did occur."

He was a very polite man and obviously he did not want to say directly that I was old.

"Yes it did," I replied.

During the rest of my stay at the camp, I stood near to where victims had been chained, just outside the ovens where they were cremated. There were a large number of ovens there. I spent many hours there praying, trying to rescue those thousands of souls who had perished under torturous conditions.

I left the Dachau camp feeling much older and very much wiser in my soul and much more compassionate in my heart. I was also able to thank my dear God, that I had been able, through the healing power that He had entrusted upon me, to help to reach out to those souls who had died there. It may come as a shock to the reader to realise that those souls who were killed in fear and torture, would remember that fear for aeons of time after their physical death. Only when the time is ripe, when their minds have reached maturity and the dawn begins to enlighten their souls, will they suddenly remember where they are and become free.

When I arrived home after my visit to Dachau, I thought that I would never want another experience of that nature, I felt very desolate and disillusioned. A few weeks later, I was in my bedroom reading a book in bed before going to sleep. Suddenly the temperature in the room dropped to what seemed zero degrees. I remember being visited by a man and a woman. The two of them pinned me down on my bed and placed a kind of iron bar around both my arms. My bed was not a bed anymore, but a wooden table on which both my arms and legs were pinned down to the table. In addition, they placed a large, circular, metallic bar around my waistline, I now realised what was happening. I was about to be tortured! I was not able to move and I knew that it was impossible to escape. I would have to endure all that they intended to do to me. I was completely at their mercy. They placed a steel helmet over my head and began to screw both sides of the helmet simultaneously. The screws were aligned with my jaw bone, so that as the screws were tightened, I was forced to open my mouth to its full extent.

With my mouth now fully open, they moved to another part of the room and brought a cardboard box towards me. It seemed to be just an ordinary shoe-box. The man placed the box close to my ears and shook it violently. I could hear that there was something inside, but I knew not what. Gradually, he opened the box and tipped its contents into my mouth, and to my horror, the box contained little mice! I cannot explain exactly the terror that I felt or the degree of fear that was in my mind. I knew that I would die! I realised that I would slowly be eaten alive. It was at this point that I realised that someone in Dachau had also undergone such a torturous experience. The victim was being released by me acting as a channel for the release of his soul.

Up to the time of writing this book (1994) I have had no further involvement with concentration camps!

Chapter Seven

MUSIC AND HEALING

Having been brought up in a musical family, I developed a deep appreciation of classical music which I have retained to this day. Today, I find myself getting more and more than ever before, with the use of music in healing. Some years ago I had been invited to Germany to participate in a healing school, in a place called Stadtenfells, near Heilbron. Incidentally, Heilbron is the twin town of Neath, South Wales, which is the nearest little town to my own village of Ystradgynlais. During this period of time there was a councillor from Neath who was attending my Sanctuary for healing. Naturally I told him that I was going away for a couple of weeks to Heilbron in Germany. Consequently, I would not be able to give him healing. He naturally mentioned that Heilbron was the twin town of Neath.

When we arrived at Bonn Airport, we were met by our various hosts and hostesses, who had invited us to stay for two days at their own homes, prior to travelling south on to Heilbron. Once again I ended up in an unusual situation, since the people whose home I had been invited to, spoke no English. Similarly I could not speak German. However, the language of love is very easily understood and I had a very harmonious time there. I also discovered that my hosts too had a deep appreciation of music. My friend Lisa Lotte Gabler said to me one day, "Would you like to visit Beethoven's home in Bonn?" I raised my hands in joy, indicating to her that I was very excited and was very much looking forward to the trip. The next day we went to Bonn and we visited Beethoven's house. That was a very joyous day for me.

In my opinion, it was Beethoven who started to open those doors that would enable me to enter the homes of the famous classical composers.

After the visit to Beethoven's home I began to feel that I had an even deeper appreciation of his music. Maybe this was because during that visit his life history was explained. It was also explained that even though Beethoven was deaf he was still able to create wonderful music.

The next time I visited Germany, I was taken on another trip, this time to Salzburg, in Austria, the birthplace of Mozart. The visit to Mozart's birthplace was also a source of joy to me. I saw his pianos, his violins and all the other precious musical instruments. Later we attended a concert of his music.

Later in life, I visited Vienna and also the various places which Beethoven, Mozart, Schubert and others had visited, the places where they had been drinking together. I also visited the house of Strauss. All in all, there were many beautiful places I visited. So I felt that between my deep love for their music, together with my visits to many of their homes, I was very close to their music. I also felt that I was able to bring the atmosphere of their homes back with me to my home, into the Sanctuary where I was healing.

I also made another visit to Austria, to a place called Eisenstadt. At that time the name of Eisenstadt did not mean anything to me at all. Whilst I was staying in Austria, our Austrian tourist guide invited some of us to go with him for a two-day sightseeing tour. It was during this tour that he took us to Eisenstadt. He took us into the local church and there we saw the organ that Beethoven had used, but which belonged to the great composer Joseph Haydn, who had written *The Creation*. A little later we visited Haydn's home, which today is a very large museum. In the museum can be seen the works of many artists who had interpreted in picture form, the wonderful scenes from *The Creation*, So, one was able to appreciate the effects of both music and colour. I would advise anyone who visits Eisenstadt that they must go and visit Haydn's home, as it is a wonderful pleasure in itself.

In their early days, before they became very famous, most well-known composers were very poor. Haydn used to invite them to his home, on one day every week, so that they could eat at least one good square meal. One day Beethoven would visit there, another day it was Mozart's turn, and so on. This also gave the composers the chance to test and interact with each other's music. I have explained all this background to you so that you get an appreciation of my very deep love for classical music and above all, its composers. Music means so much to me in my healing work. I feel that it helps to unfold the many disorders and disharmonies that can lie in the mind. Today, I love to combine music and healing. Music opens up the souls, the hearts and the minds of both men and women. I have also seen its effect upon little children. I remember a child coming to see me in my Sanctuary at home. I used to play some records during the healing. One day he decided to bring one of his own records to play.

He said, "Please play this music while you heal."

I placed it on the record player's turntable and this is what it played: *I want to teach the world to sing.*

He wanted it played over and over again. I never tired of it. I tried to see the effect through the child's eyes. Alas, the child never made it through life. He passed on into the higher realms of spirit. He gave me such a smile the last time I saw him. Did the healing fail? Some people would have said so. No! Healing opened the door to a wider understanding. That child, like other patients who die, was being prepared to go into the mansions of which Jesus spoke. Many people will disagree with this point. But I do not care what they say. I know that I have found a spiritual jewel in the crown. No one can take it from me, and my cup runneth over with the numerous recollections in my memory closet and I can remember those events that I have witnessed. That little child passed over and was received. He was no stranger when he arrived there. There will be many people who will go into the spirit world with 'L' plates on their backs. They will not know the way. It is a great pity, because we have so much to give, so much to share and so many to enlighten. Those who try to deny the very truths that we give unto others, must try to understand. Perhaps they do not want to listen. Perhaps it frightens them! Perhaps they think it weird. Perhaps it is that they do not wish to receive such knowledge. Then we are not all of the same make up, are we? But I thank God for the numerous experiences that I have had, walking hand in hand with him. Knowing that in giving, we are receiving. In receiving, we share. In sharing, we build up a great wall of understanding, secure in our minds, bodies and souls, reaching out to that great and wonderful world that is ahead of us. A great world brought close to me by my very dear friend, Raheede.

During one of my visits to Salzburg, I met a very interesting lady. Her Christian name was Inca, unfortunately I cannot remember her surname. This lady had a unique type of involvement with Spirit. She was the proud owner of a small hammer. With this she was able to tap various objects, and in her mind, she was able to tell if these objects were in harmony with their surroundings. For example, she could strike a small rock which she held in her hand and depending how that sound would resonate in her mind, she was able to find the causes of the various pains people suffered.

In many ways Inca reminded me of Moses the prophet in *The Old Testament*. Moses was the person who led his people when they were fleeing from the Egyptians. When they came across the obstacle of the Red Sea, it was Moses who raised his arms resulting in the parting of the water, thus permitting a pathway for his followers to escape. After safe passage through the parted waters he was able once again to allow them to close, thus preventing his enemies from pursuing them.

So it can be seen that Inca had similar abilities to Moses, but in a more minor way. Although Inca never charged for her healing work, she did receive many large monetary gifts from various patients. For example, some people who consulted her were industrialists. They would ask her to find out if the land which they were about to purchase was suitable for building upon; was there any likelihood of subsidence from underground waterways? Inca was always found to be accurate. If she discovered a problem she would advise them to build on another part of the land so that they would not encounter any building problems.

On my fourth visit to Salzburg, Inca was taken very seriously ill. She became hospitalised and she asked me if I would pay her a visit, so I went to see her. During my visit, she held the hammer in between her hand and mine. She told me that in this way she was able to assess the healing power that flowed through my hand into her body. This lasted for about ten seconds. When she counted to ten she withdrew her hand from mine and thanked me very gratefully for what I had done for her. Then she kissed my hand. She turned to me and said, "I will be gone just after the stroke of midnight, at ten seconds after midnight I shall be gone."

Shortly after I left, I discovered that she had lapsed into a coma and died very peacefully. The lady in the next bed to her had been instructed by Inca to make sure that just after the stroke of midnight, she was to check that she was dead. It was indeed about ten seconds after midnight that she was confirmed to be dead.

Before her death she had asked me to attend the funeral. I was very privileged to do that. There was a wonderful warmth of feeling at the cemetery that day. All her friends and many of the industrialists that she had helped were there. Such was the respect that they had for her. Since her death, Inca has returned to me in spirit about three or four times.

Each time quite powerfully and each time she brought the hammer with her. She still uses the hammer even on the other side of life. I will always hold her in very high esteem.

Some years ago, I had another unusual experience. It happened when I was attending a seminar in England. I can't remember who the medium was, but I very clearly remember that he was able to play the piano and worked with mentally retarded children. In one of the classes that formed part of the seminar, there was a patient there who no one could communicate with. We were however, able to bathe, feed, and clothe him. He was a very uncommunicative person, and he kept himself to himself. He held in his hand a small piece of wood that was in the form of a small peg. He always kept this with him and he would never allow himself to be parted from it, either during the day or the night. At night he kept it under his pillow. There was obviously something very significant to him about this simple piece of wood. I very often thought about what the relevance was. Could it be that he had some connection with carpentry, or had his parents, grandparents, or friend given it to him? I did not know.

One day this medium told me about a man who was attending one of his classes. Suddenly he raised his head when some of Chopin's music was being played. This music must have touched some chord in his mind, for it caused him to say the first few words that he had ever spoken during the whole seminar.

Over the years, I came into contact with that medium on a few occasions. The last time I saw him, he informed me that the man was continuing to make very good progress. He progressed to the stage where he was able to play the drums, and then he became a very good judge of the correct tempo or beat of music.

This short story takes me back to the time of the Scriptures where it is written: 'and the trumpet shall sound and the dead shall be raised from iniquity.' This implies that the trumpet is capable of making a loud sound, and just as the bugler who plays the *Last Post*, it is capable of touching a chord in people's hearts, minds and souls.

Many years ago, my colleague and niece, Gwenda Jones, was able, through her Egyptian Guide, Ali Ashmood, to activate physical phenomena. Raheede used to refer to Ali Ashmood as one of the sons of the desert. He also said the desert was capable of producing many things. Although it consists mainly of sand and stone, it was capable during the early Christian times of bringing much enlightenment. Just like the sand on the seashores of today, the desert sand is capable of bringing wonderful vibrations to those people who touch it. It can be very useful in developing the psychic faculties. This can be done by first obtaining a small cardboard box about twelve to fourteen inches square and filling it with sand to the depth of about six to eight inches. If you place your hands into the sand, it is possible under spirit guidance to achieve physical vibrations, which in turn can generate thought patterns in the mind. It can even give a tremendous awareness of happenings during Egyptian times. I do not know exactly how this works, it is a bit of a mystery to me. A mystery which is similar to the power which is within the pyramid. No one really knows how the pyramids were built or how this energy is generated.

I find that when I touch the sand, I am capable of becoming a kind of sand reader. During these sand readings, it is possible to foretell the future from the thought patterns that are impressed upon the mind. I can assure you that these images are quite clear and there is nothing sinister about it at all. The effect is similar to that obtained when you place an empty shell to the ear. One is able to sense the sound of the waves of the sea. I was informed by the Guides many years ago, that if a deaf person, or a person who suffers from tinnitus, were to listen to the soothing sounds of the waves produced by placing a shell to the ear, it can bring about either an improvement in hearing or produce a soothing effect which can reduce the discomfort of the noises.

The use of sea-sand seems to combine the energies of both the sand and the sea. Sand-packs were sometimes used by the late Edgar Cayce, the famous American, who was able to diagnose and prescribe treatments for various diseases, whilst in the trance state. He was sometimes called the "Sleeping Prophet". He was born in Hopkinsville, Kentucky, in 1877. He died in 1945, in Virginia. In 1931, the Association for Research and Enlightenment Inc., (A.R.E.) was formed. This association was primarily formed to record and catalogue all the readings and teachings that were meticulously recorded during Cayce's lifetime. As a child, Edgar Cayce found that he had extraordinary powers. At the age of eleven years, when he was reading his Bible one day, in a special tree-house he had made for himself on his father's farm, an angel appeared to him and said, "Your wish has been granted; what is it that you would like most in your life?" Edgar answered, "My wish is to be able to help people, but especially children." The angel then disappeared. From this position he was helped and guided to realise his goals. During his life he became famous for his diagnostic abilities and the obscure treatments that he would give out during his 'readings' in the trance state. When he lost his voice as a young man, he was only able to cure it by getting a friend of his to help him give and record his first major reading. Later on, some doctors came to him to request help for their patients. However, most people visited him privately, with complaints that usually defined the medical profession. Often he was able to diagnose what was wrong with them and prescribe curative treatments.

Whilst he was working in the A.R.E. he prescribed sand-pack treatments for some of his patients. The nurses who worked at the A.R.E. would have to take some patients down to the beach and pack hot sand around their bodies which had been wetted with sea-water. His readings said that the sand at Virginia Beach had a high gold content and was highly radioactive.

Let us now compare these experiences with my situation today, where I am involved with other good souls – the musical composers. The number of times I have sat and listened to the music of Beethoven, Mozart, Mendelssohn, Haydn, Liszt, or Chopin, I have long since forgotten. One night these composers appeared in my Sanctuary, I could see their figures so clearly, so I enquired of my Guide who these people were, I wanted to know the purpose of their presence. They, of course had been drawn to the beauty of their music that I had been playing. Now how could their lovely music be related to the suffering of people? Their music could create new thought patterns in the mind, which in turn could develop into a betterment in their physical health.

Suddenly, in the corner of the room, I saw another man, whose head was bowed down, he seemed full of sadness and was forlorn. I again enquired of my Guide who this person was. He replied that it was Wagner. The Guide said Wagner was very dejected since he thought that he would never be able to say that his creative music would ever be used to heal sick people. He was always aware of the fact that his music had been used during the torturing of many thousands of people and at mass exterminations at concentration camps.

I began to ask myself what could be done to help him. I thought something had to be done, but I did not know how this could be brought about. Then I realised the best way to help him, was by using his music in healing. I thought this would surely give him pleasure, and who knows, his music may be able to perform an act of healing. At one moment his music can be beautiful, so harmonious and creative, and yet in the next moment it can become so violent and so clearly expresses the tortuous states of the mind. I told myself, it had to be done.

Later, I remembered the time when I was at Burgstadtenfells, near Heilbron in Germany, when I was one of the speakers who was taking part in a week's School of Healing. I was giving a lecture on Music and Healing. I asked myself how I could give such a lecture without mentioning Wagner's name. I knew that the mentioning of his name was too delicate a subject for the German students who were attending the School. Then I realised that one has to face up to the truth and accept the consequences of whatever comes one's way. Consequently I mentioned to them that it was a great shame that Wagner's name had been associated with so much misery and that he would never be able to have the pleasure of knowing that his creative music could be used to heal the sick. So I informed them that I had decided that I would introduce them to his music and we would see what would happen.

At the end of the School, it was a Sunday morning, we all gathered together to say our farewells to each other. Before I left I was presented with a gift which was in a very large box. I asked what the gift was. The presenter of the gift was named Herr Smug, he was a Heil Pracktiker who lived in Munich. He said, through the interpreter, "Open it and see for yourself. But take care, it is very heavy."

So they brought me a little table and placed the large box on it so that I could open it up with ease. When I opened the box, there before my eyes was a box of the three operas that Wagner had written: *The Flying Dutchman, Parsifal,* and *Tannhäuser.*

Since then, *Tannhäuser* has proved to be invaluable to me in my healing work. Through this work, Wagner has helped to restore serenity to the minds which were in a chaotic state and imbalance, which had been present for a long time; the imbalance between the subconscious and the conscious mind. I have utilised *Tannhäuser* in various workshops, seminars, and also in my own private Sanctuary. It is always a source of joy to me when I remember that night when I first saw Wagner. Today, I am also very happy to have the knowledge that as a result of using his music in healing, Wagner enjoys a better state of mind in the Spirit World.

When I mention this fact, most people are reduced to a state of silence. They either accept this statement, or they don't. On one occasion when I was taking part in a seminar in Southport, England, I asked the parents of a child who had died at Mauthausen, what they had felt when I played

Tannhäuser. The mother said that she wanted to get up and walk out of the room, but I felt that she was chained to her chair and was unable to move. She felt she was being forced to listen to the music. As she spoke, I could see the tears running down her face, I could see that she too was experiencing a healing.

Beethoven's music is the music that can release locked joints. The vibrations are able to disperse the adhesions that tend to collect around arthritic joints. His music can also correct slipped discs and poker-back conditions. When I work with Beethoven's music I feel that I am able to manipulate the spine into certain positions that are required by the spirit doctors who work with us, so that a very big improvement or a cure can be brought about. I have also utilised his music for treating blindness, deafness and head noises.

Mozart's music can be used whenever there is a lowness of spirit; for those who feel dejected and oppressed. His music can also be used for treating all forms of skin diseases such as dermatitis, psoriasis, eczema, and even warts can be cured. His music is able to reach those inner parts of the soul, especially in cases where patients want to follow a religious quest, but feel that they have put themselves outside the laws of God. They are searching for God but feel they have lost their way. The various Masses that Mozart wrote are able to steer them along the right path to the highest point that the mind and the soul can reach.

Mozart's wonderful inspirational music, such as the *Ave Verum,* I find particularly good in helping people with disturbances of the mind. His Andante movement in the *No. 21 Piano Concerto* is especially good for helping those who have suffered emotional pain, such as grief.

Haydn's work is of tremendous importance in Spiritual matters, it has the ability to awaken the soul. The opening bars of *The Creation* are especially useful for this. There is something so special about his musical work; I feel that it can open the pineal gland, thus enabling entry into the subconscious mind. Wagner's music has the same effect. It can help to erase from the mind the memories of the brutalities that were inflicted on those poor souls who suffered so much in the concentration camps. Today, some of the world-famous conductors, such as Daniel Barenboim, who is a Jew, and André Previn, are able to introduce Wagner's music to the people of Israel. Many of the victims of the camps went to Israel in the hope of finally finding true peace. Barenboim was heckled by the audience, on one occasion in 1991, when he was playing Wagner's music to the people of Tel Aviv. He pleaded with them not to blame Wagner, as he cannot be blamed for those atrocities. In my own mind I am certain that many of Wagner's discordant notes such as those that can be heard in the *Flying Dutchman, Tannhäuser,* and *Parsifal* could help solve the mystery that surrounds A.I.D.S.

I had not been much involved in Wagner's music, not until I had been concerned with the concentration camps. In my early days I was not aware that music could be used in healing. However, I did feel a very strong association with most of the composers. Either, I was seeking them, or, they were seeking me. Later, I realised that it was the composers who were seeking me. They appeared to me in spirit form in my Sanctuary, often they were seen grouped together. Through my Guide, Raheede, I was told who they were and how they had been drawn to the harmonious vibrations that were there. It was indeed a joy to me.

Wagner first appeared to me in my Sanctuary on the same night that I first saw the other composers, he, however, was apart from the others. They were separated by disharmony. Not that there was disharmony between Wagner and the others such as Haydn, Bach, Mozart, Beethoven, Schubert, and Liszt. The disharmony existed because Wagner felt that he would never be able to attain the level of appreciation for his music that the others had. He felt that their music could always be heard being played in churches, sanctuaries, theatres, etc. He felt that his music had been ostracised because it was played when the prisoners first arrived at those terrible camps.

Today I intermix Wagner's music with that of the other composers. I find that their music can be used together in harmony. This has meant too, that Wagner's music can be used very powerfully in helping mental disorders such as epilepsy, those who are in despair, or those whose minds are in disorder and twisted. I find that the use of Wagner's music, which is also twisted, distorted and mysterious, is able to penetrate the minds of such people and help them.

In the future, I feel that music is going to play a very important part in healing. Today it is used very powerfully to help those suffering from autism. Presently there are over two hundred and fifty Music Therapists in this country (U.K.). Elton John was so impressed with the music therapy that he spends some of his time raising funds. One of my remaining ambitions in life is to expose patients to the combined energies of both music and colour. I will do as much research as I possibly can into this subject.

I also envisage that the field of healing will have a brilliant future and

I am certain that my precious colleagues who presently work with me will be able to touch the 'hem of that Divine garment' and as a result, many great things will be achieved. But as always, someone has to start. Healing starts with the 'Laying on of Hands' and with 'Distant Healing', but the future experimentation will soon begin in a very big way. At our Sanctuary, we will begin by exposing patients to both colour and music. My dear friend, Wayne Jones, will have a great future with the scientific aspects of Spiritual Healing. Presently he has been guided to learn the German language, and some day he will be able to utilise this knowledge to give lectures to the German races in their mother tongue. I am sure that he will work with me and demonstrate other experiments of various kinds.

My involvement with music has increased a lot and I know that there has to be a slight change. For example, I find the Rock Gospel type of music can also help to heal the troubled mind. The potentials of music are always there to be used, but we are only touching the fringes of healing. What do we know about healing? What have we learnt about healing? I think Jesus puts it very aptly when he says:

'Marvel not at the things that I do, greater things than this ye shall do, because I go unto my Father.'

The healers of the future will be able to carry on from where we have left off today, building new structures of thinking, and we will be able to achieve things that we were not able to do before. Harry Edwards was the greatest healer since the time of Jesus Christ, that I am certain of. I can only marvel and reflect upon the beauty of the energy radiated through that man's hands, mind and soul. For my own part, I can safely say that I will be able to work in my Father's house long after my earthly life has ended. I never, never want to detach myself from my loved ones who are performing the healing. The healers that I have trained are not merely friends, they are my beloved family; my God-given family, and I am certain that I will never ever leave their side, I will always draw nearer to them and help them. Whatever I may learn, and I am sure that I will continue to learn, I will impart that knowledge to them in no small terms.

Real life stories

For years Harry Bater had been in and out of hospital as doctors tried unsuccessfully to halt the gradual deterioration of his spine. Eventually he survived on pain killers and a surgical corset. But by then he had also developed arthritis of the spine, hips and knees.

Then in 1975, after six treatments from spiritual healer Marian Butler, Harry discarded both corset and drugs and was free from pain.

"I only asked for treatment for my arthritis." Harry said, "but Miss Butler put her hands on me and said I also had pain from a spine defect. She gave the same clinical diagnosis that X-rays had revealed."

Marian Butler has been healing for over 30 years now and still lives in her childhood home, a terraced cottage in the Welsh village of Ystradgynlais.

She was aware of psychic abilities as a child: "But in a strict chapel family you didn't mention hearing and seeing things not apparent to others."

When she was 30 she sat at the bedside of a young cousin who was dying. "I asked God to grant the sort of healing we read about in the New Testament. Immediately the boy showed signs of recovery."

The local doctor couldn't explain it; but the news spread. Now Marian Butler is vice-president of the World Federation of Healing.

Most of her cases are chronic. Mrs. Glenys Davies had been treated for varicose ulcers for nearly 30 years – but they always returned. In despair she went to Marian: two months later her worst ulcer had healed.

Marian Butler believes that to obtain a lasting cure you must treat the patient as a whole: "This involves the body, the mind and the spirit."

She also believes that many people are unrecognised healers, but to learn to use their gift they must be trained. She learnt from the late Harry Edwards and Gordon Turner.

No scientific research into spiritual healing has been done in this country, but many of Marian's patients feel tremendous heat as she treats them.

"Healing does often manifest itself as heat," agreed Marian. "I believe it comes from God." She doesn't claim spiritual healing can always cure; but says it can always help.

For further information, write to : National Federation of Spiritual Healers. Old Manor Farm, Church Street, Sunbury on Thames, Middlesex TW16. enclosing an s.a.e., or phone: Sunbury 83164.

Muscle power – new approach to natural health

The body, says Natalie Davenport, is a remarkable instrument that knows whether it's well or not. Natalie is a practitioner of a new approach to natural health called Touch For Health, whereby she test the muscles of the body in a certain way to get an indication of any imbalances.

The method stems from the work of an American chiropractor, George Goodheart, who discovered that tension and muscle spasm could be treated by strengthening the opposite, weak, muscles rather than working directly with the tight muscle itself. Simple tests detect energy imbalances, muscle weakness, postural defects, reactions to food and drink. Touch For Health then suggests therapies such as massage, acupressure and diet changes.

Natalie came to the method after many years practising spiritual healing. Now she feels she has found a system that she can accept.

"It is objective," she says, "whereas all the other techniques were far more subjective and intuitive. Here for the first time I met a system where the patient was getting the same feedback as the person doing the healing. Touch For Health has a very precise series of tests, a precise series of treatments and a precise result.

"The body can tell us what's wrong with us if we just look at it. By the way it is carried, by its colour or smell, its gestures and what it eats."

One example of success was a woman who was so ill the hospital said she was dying.

"When I did the muscle-testing I couldn't find anything basically wrong. Everything responded; but at a lower level than it should, although the woman's body wasn't diseased.

"It turned out that she'd been to an Indian community, desperate to find something of value – but found this wasn't the way. Her will to live had

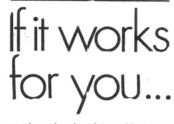

If it works for you...

An ex-miner who pin-points problem areas by massaging the foot . . . a Welsh lady with laser-like healing power . . . Don't believe it? It may be weird, but it seems to work

been sapped, but as soon as she was able to admit this to herself there was a marked change in her colour and pulse.

"By muscle-testing we found she needed a new diet, some acupuncture, plus physical balancing and counselling. After three weeks she was well on the way to recovery."

Touch For Health doesn't take the place of orthodox medicine. "It doesn't diagnose, so in that sense it isn't healing." explains Natalie, "but it's a tool by which you can measure your own health. You can learn to listen to your own body."

For more information, s.a.e. to: Administrative Representatives, 29 Bushey Close, High Wycombe, Bucks.

Foot treatment stands up to the sceptics

Reflexology, or zone therapy, used to be dismissed as cranky and unscientific. But now orthodox doctors are gradually becoming less sceptical.

The system works on the idea that there are 10 electrical zones running through the body, terminating in such places as ears, tongue, back, hands and feet. When you are in superb health these impulses run freely; but when you are ill they become clogged up. The blocked-up impulses are felt as pain when any of the terminal areas are massaged correctly. Most therapists choose to work with the feet – they are the easiest areas to massage, are sensitive to pain and are good indicators of general health.

One of the leading practitioners is Joseph Corvo a Yorkshireman who used to be a miner. Though medically untrained he has practised with great success for 25 years, although he does not claim to cure illnesses.

"But the treatment can help anybody to get well and stay well," he said. "What happens is that we eat far too many foods that are high in acids. Deep foot massage frees the unwanted acids from the nerve endings and eliminates them from the body."

All bodily organs, according to reflexologists, tie up with particular areas in the feet – anything wrong with the liver is felt in the ball of the foot, while the state of ears and eyes is felt in the toes.

Most illnesses can benefit from this form of treatment, but reflexologists point out that you don't have to be ill to benefit from therapy. "It acts as an early warning system," said Ken Holne, a psychologist who runs clinics and training courses at the Churchill Centre, London.

A GP said: "I wouldn't trust it as an alternative to orthodox medicine for every complaint, but it certainly can't do any harm."

For further information, send an s.a.e. to The Churchill Centre, 22 Montagu Street, London W1.

Books to read: The Miracle Of You, £2.95 inc. p & p., and The Best Is Yet To Come, £4.95 inc. p & p., both by Joseph Corvo, Bedford Books. 33 Wickham Avenue. Croydon CR0 8TZ; Reflexology Today, by Doreen Bayley. £3.90 inc. p. & p.. from the Humane Education Centre. Avenue Lodge, Bounds Green Road, London N22.

Joseph Corvo: not promising cures, just better health

One of the more 'honest' press cuttings.

105

Chapter Eight

SPIRITUAL HEALING EXPLAINED

When I holidayed in California in April, 1976, I was invited by the Rev. Doug Henderson onto his evening radio show which he called his *Parson to Person* show, on K.N.E.W. Radio, Oakland. As a guest on his show I was asked to talk about Spiritual Healing. Later in the show listeners were invited to ring in and ask me questions. I have included this radio interview in this book because the Rev. Henderson asked many of the questions that most people ask me about Spiritual Healing. He introduced me to his listeners and then began to ask me the following questions:

D.H.   We are very happy to have you with us, I understand your subject is Spiritual Healing.

M.B.   Yes, and I have been practising this now for twenty-eight years, and during this period I have seen some very wonderful things take place.

D.H.   You prefer to use the phrase 'Spiritual Healing' rather than 'Faith Healing'?

M.B.   Yes, and I am a member of the National Federation of Spiritual Healers.

D.H.   Tell us about your work and what you do, and also about the World Federation of Healers.

M.B.   I have a Healing Sanctuary where I treat between one-hundred-and-forty to one-hundred-and-sixty patients per week. In the U.K. we are free to practise Spiritual Healing because we have had legislation passed in our parliamentary system to allow us to operate and also to perform healing in the hospitals. We, however, ask and seek the co-operation of the doctor in charge.

D.H.   Do you do your healing by the 'Laying on of Hands'?

M.B.   Yes. I don't only practise the 'Laying on of Hands' through prayer, but I also practise 'Distant' or 'Absent Healing' through prayer as well. That means that I am in communication with patients who write to me or telephone me.

D.H.   Maybe later on in our programme tonight, we will invite listeners to call in, who may have some particular needs.

M.B.   If I can be of any service to them I shall only be too glad to do so.

D.H.   All right. You say that you work with hospitals sometimes and the physicians actually call on you. Under what circumstances would that happen?

M.B.   Yes. If a patient who is in hospital requests Spiritual Healing whilst under the jurisdiction of the medical profession, they simply ask the physician in charge of their case, if a healer can be invited into the hospital. Invariably, perhaps in nine cases out of ten, permission is granted and we go in and treat them.

D.H.   And you do this by the 'Laying on of Hands' and by praying for them?

M.B.   Yes. We do precisely that.

D.H.   Tell us something about the National Federation of Spiritual Healers, and the World Federation of Healing.

M.B.   The National Federation of Spiritual Healers has recently celebrated their twenty-first anniversary. We have grouped together people who have the healing gift, irrespective of religious denomination or colour or creed. We number about four thousand members at present. There are also associate members, who like to link up with our movement but are not themselves healers.

D.H.   What training must a person have? Or should I put it to you this way: can anybody do this; shall we say a devoted Christian? How do you get to become a healer?

M.B.   First of all, the desire must be there to serve humanity, when we do it through prayer. You must remember that I am not the *healer*, I am only a *healing channel* through which the healing takes place. I pray to God and His healing power flows through me to the patient. The main training that is necessary is to become accustomed to treating sick people. The desire must first be there, but in my opinion, it is principally a gift sent from God to those who are desirous of helping those who are sick.

D.H. Are you saying then that it is only possible for some people to become healers but it is not possible for every Christian?

M.B. I am not saying that someone who is a Christian cannot practise the art of Spiritual Healing, but first they must be sufficiently in attunement with God through prayer. They must ask, and then they will receive His help. There are those who work in this field daily and their powers are that much greater because they are practising it all the time. Anyone could do it, provided that they have the love of God in their hearts.

D.H. Would you liken it to musical ability? That is, if you really have a feel for it and practise it?

M.B. Yes. It is a natural gift.

D.H. Now tell us a little about what you have been doing in California.

M.B. I first of all came out to California for a holiday, and I have been here for about a month. During this period I came into contact with some very nice people who invited me into their Methodist Church in Palo Alto, to give a lecture on Spiritual Healing. Although I had not met them before, it felt as if I had known them all my life.

D.H. You know the Methodist Church started in your country but flourished even more here in this country. I say that modestly because I am one of them. So you have given some lectures and Healing Services have you?

M.B In California you mean? Yes, I have given one talk on Spiritual Healing but I did not give any healing in the Church. But we did form a meditation group there. We sat quietly to attune with God so that we could draw the best that we could from Him, so that we could all feel the inflow of Divine love coming into us.

D.H. In our land, when one talks of Spiritual Healing there is always the danger of hearing someone say that he is a 'quack', or he is trying to make a lot of money out of it, or he is manipulating people. How do you handle that, or feel about it?

M.B. I feel very deeply about it because I have not charged anyone a penny in my whole life. I would be afraid to charge, lest I should lose the wonderful gift that God has bestowed upon me. Spiritual Healing is free. I have received it freely and so I give it freely to others. But there are others who do charge, but I am not their judge.

D.H. Of course, a person who is doing the things that you are doing is kind of in the horns of a dilemma. They do not want to charge for a healing, yet they have to somehow make enough money to support themselves. How do you manage this?

M.B. Fortunately I am not in that category, because I have limited private means, for I am senior citizen in the U.K. and I get a small pension from the State. I do not make any money out of healing.

D.H. What about offerings or gifts?

M.B. Offerings and money are accepted for the upkeep of the church. We also have a church committee and its officers deal with this. My job primarily is to preach the gospel and to heal the sick.

D.H. What kinds of things can you heal?

M.B. We treat all manner of disease, for example Rheumatoid Arthritis, Multiple Sclerosis, Nervous Tension, Migraine, Skin Diseases such as Dermatitis, Psoriasis or Eczema, Epilepsy; it covers a very wide range of disease. We treat all kinds of patients.

D.H. Do you make any distinction in healing between those things that we may call 'organic' and that which we my call 'functional'? Functional diseases being something that malfunctions in the body, while organic, being something that is wrong, for example, fractured. Do you make such distinctions like that?

M.B. No, not really. As I have said, I do practise the 'Laying on of Hands' but I also practise 'Absent' or 'Distant Healing' as well. As I have said, I am not the healer, God is the healer and his healing power flows through me. It is immaterial if the problem is organic, inorganic, or of a psychosomatic nature. We feel that through God's Divine Healing Intelligence, He is able to see right through to the direct cause of the disease. Through the 'Laying on of Hands', we are able to transmit the healing energy that comes from God. The success rate with all diseases is very high indeed.

D.H. I suppose this question is always thrown at you, but what do you do in the case of a broken bone? Can you do an instant healing on a broken bone?

M.B. Oh no. But we do co-operate with the medical profession. We have never claimed within the National Federation of Spiritual

Healing that we are an alternative to medical treatment. We are not, but we are highly complementary to it. Patients who may be severely injured, we may advise them to seek medical help through surgery. In which case we would pray for them while they are in hospital. This gives them the opportunity of combining both therapies and receiving the best that both treatments can give.

D.H.   Thank you, and now I am going to open the phones to our listeners.

Later there followed about ten phone calls from listeners in Berkeley, Oakland, San Francisco, San Jose, and Santa Rosa areas, concerning pregnancy, dyslexia, throat cancer, benign head tumours, hernia, urinary infection, nervous tension, over weight, and spinal injury (whiplash). Finally, a lady asked for prayers for her two sons who were working in the Edgar Cayce Foundation (Association of Research and Enlightenment, Inc.) in Virginia Beach, Virginia. I closed the radio show in prayer by asking God for help for all those listeners who rang in to the show.

I would like to explain to you about the various aspects of Spiritual Healing. Many people today know what Spiritual Healing is all about. Unfortunately, there are still millions of people in the world to whom this is not the case. It therefore becomes necessary for us as mediums or channels for Spiritual Healing to try to enlighten the masses and thereby lead them into avenues where they can be helped spiritually. Spiritual Healing embraces the healing of the body, mind and spirit. When we turn to the spiritual world in order to receive higher spiritual help, we must first prepare ourselves for that attunement that enables us to communicate through empathy, love and compassion. This in turn enables us to restore health to those who need our help.

First, we must withdraw into the silence within ourselves. We then turn to Almighty God or to The Supreme Being, if you prefer to call him by this name. What we like to think of here is what is known as the Healing Intelligence. It is an intelligent power which is able to penetrate to the root-cause cause of the sickness or disease. We are then able to witness how perfect healing comes about, when a healing of the physical body had been aimed for. Spiritual Healing is able to do, today far more than medical science has to offer. This is simply because, in general, traditional medicine only treats the symptoms. However, before a healing can take place, the causes, first of all have to be removed.

Of course, we must realise that most diseases are of a psychosomatic origin. When we are able to make contact with the spiritual world, we open our mental channels to embrace the objective which we hope to achieve, that is, to encompass and to embrace ourselves with this deep feeling and the earnest desire of expressing God's love in its entirety. When we do decide to prepare ourselves as channels, to render Spiritual Healing to patients, the first thing we must do, is to align ourselves with the spiritual mind of the patient, who God has sent to us. These healers are known as the Healing Guides. Without these spiritual guides, we are not able to accomplish anything.

Shall we for a moment pause to assess what causes illness in the first place. We must recognise that fear plays an important part and is one of the main reasons for maladjustment, causing various illnesses in the physical body. Anxiety and fear in themselves are contrary to God's laws. God did not place fear in the human mind or soul. The teachings of Jesus tells us to 'fear not', this simply says that we should always have positive thoughts. Since when we think positively, we create wonderful vibrations, creative in the most perfect sense. The world in which we live today arouses great fear in the minds of many people. Sometimes fear arises through conflict in the family, or we are afraid of neighbours or the general influence of the society in which we live. Then there is fear of the opinion of others, who may be thinking ill of us, not to mention the fear of what the future holds for us as individuals or as nations. For example, there is fear of the possibility of wars. When we look at the world scene today, we can envisage the fears that are being fostered in the minds of those who are engaged in war. We who act as mediums or channels for healing should aspire to rid ourselves of all fear, and turn to the spiritual world to receive the inflow of the Divine energies, which are creative and always to the end, perfect, right and true. As I have said previously, we recognise that most diseases of the physical body are caused by fear. Those fears affect the mind, which in turn can affect and disturb the metabolism of the physical body. These latent desires which have become suppressed, can in turn cause repressions and repercussions in the physical body.

If we can incorporate, at all times, both Spiritual Healing and medical science for the benefit of all mankind, a wonderful state of well-being can be received by all of us. I envisage in years to come, great activity in the spiritual field directed toward mankind. Spiritual Healing is not only confined to the treatment and curing of diseases of the physical body, it can also be utilised to restore serenity and happiness to others. It will necessitate all of us aiming towards that high spiritual path to success, in order to bring about that wonderful peace on earth that Jesus spoke of. I know that all the things that we have available to help mankind, involve tremendous efforts on the mental resources of the healing channel or medium. There has to be a period of time when we must try to understand and be 'in tune' with the needs and wishes of the patient. In a great many cases this can be very difficult. But when we reach to that Divine Intelligence, it can open up channels of thought or perceptions in the mind of the healer, so as to enable the basic cause of the illness or disease to be perceived. Some mediums will want to research continually so that they can progress and achieve the ultimate good that they are capable of. Not all healing channels can or will want to aspire to the same heights. Some will be satisfied with prayer and the 'Laying on of Hands'. Others will want to progress further and will want to research deeper into the scientific spiritualness of mankind.

It should also be realised that it is not only mankind who can benefit from Spiritual Healing or the direct intercessions that healers have to offer. It can also be directed toward the animal kingdom or toward plant life or to the soil upon which we tread. Since all these things are part of God, healing, which is of the Divine, can come from only one source, and that source is God. God is good. God is merciful. What gives me such joy and happiness is that no matter what we have done, which may be bad, or we may feel sorry about, we can stop, retrace our steps and start all over again. Eventually a change comes about in our being and we find that we are able to receive the very best of help.

Spiritual Healing can work through many levels and no one has a monopoly on it. It's given to all of us to become healing channels. All we need to do is to radiate a strong smile from our faces to those who we meet on life's pathway. We can also radiate healing through music. I use music very often in my own healing environment.

For me, spiritual healing is an energy that comes from God. An energy which is full of creative beauty. For example, just think of a man and wife who love each other and are not able to have children. When they turn to us as 'mediums' so to speak, we are able to grasp the situation and trace the reason for their problems and establish why conception and pregnancy is not possible. Very often, it is sufficient only to correct a small thing and then they will be blessed with a child in their own home.

A wonderful intelligence is at work here which our heart recognises and which is able to influence our mind and body. Then it shows us how it can effect the harmony and health in the physical state, through the energy and love bestowed on us.

I like to advise patients, I do it without fail every day, so that when they get up and look in the mirror, they should present each other with a smile that will influence the whole day. The day will then run more harmoniously. Look at the simple things in life. Just look at nature, and look for beauty in all things; the beauty that emanates from the flowers and the trees. Look at the wonderful colours and patterns. At night we can look to the heavens and observe the patterns that are constantly changing in the universe. We can all be in harmony with the universe that God has made. We can become consciously aware of the reservoir of energy that emanates from our midst and we can place our entire being in God's wonderful care and keeping, knowing that we are in harmony with ourselves and nature. We can then be assured of the tremendous harmony that can be created between ourselves and our Maker. I would strongly advise all patients to try to get to know their inner being; the real you. Do not suppress your feelings, let your wonderful thoughts flow in the correct way. Think of each new day as being better than the day before. Since if we restore harmony to the mind, then I know with certainty that harmony can also be improved in the physical body. Love is the energy of the Creator. If we love ourselves, then we must learn to share that love with others with whom we mix in our homes or meet in our daily lives. If we love each other then we are perfecting the universal law. The law of giving, the law of creating. With this law we can all carry on with life's path, by stating that we love God. When we love God, it is not always necessary to utilise long words or obscure phraseology or to cover ourselves in self-aggrandisement, in order to obtain higher achievements with God. It does not work like that. It is what we feel that really matters. It is the love that we share. It is the compassion that we need to show to all in this wonderful universe in which we have been created.

To me, Spiritual Healing is a gigantic subject that can be utilised in many different ways. I would like to think that through the directive thoughts of love that we harbour, we are able to radiate this love to the world that is around and about us. Remember this one very important fact: What you think, can be picked up by someone, somewhere, at any time. It can be utilised by those who need it most. So by sending out our thoughts to all corners of the earth and even the planets, if life exists there, for the ultimate good, man can become reconciled with his Maker. Such positive directed thought is also used in 'Absent' or 'Distant Healing'. Be happy and free. Free from fear, free from anxiety, free from worry, free from despair, and always look to the hills and mountains from whence cometh our help and strength, as it can come from God.

When I discuss Spiritual Healing, it is insufficient just to find out if the person can be helped. It does not satisfy me spiritually that they get better – although I am always very pleased and grateful to spirit or to God. I always want to know why Spiritual Healing sometimes fails. For a long time I have always wanted to understand the so-called 'incurable cases' – those cases where the doctors and modern science fail to come up with the answers. Modern medicine fails not because it cannot treat the physical body but because the cause has nothing to do with physical symptoms. It may be due to some trauma in a person's life, it may even be due to something they brought into this life from a previous life. Jesus says in the Bible: 'You cannot treat the patient . . . Ye not until the third and fourth generation.'

The illness may even be due to a deep emotional upset, for example, a divorce or the death of a loved one. It may be due to fear; fear of darkness or even fear of what people think of them. It may be due to worry, debt or bankruptcy. I sight these purely as examples to illustrate the numerous causes of disease that have nothing to do directly with the physical body. Doctors rarely understand, or want to understand, the diagnosis and the symptoms that Spiritual Healers get from the Spirit Doctors. So if I am treating a child that is mentally defective, I find that working on that mind is a very difficult thing in itself. One must always try and dig deeper and deeper so as to find the true causes of the illness. Almost in every case where I have had time to study not only the symptoms but also the personality of the patient, some great revelations come to light that have a significant effect on the illness. The doctor may be treating a patient only on the physical level, and the patient is not responding, but they will not stop to think that the cause may be due to the fact that the problems may stem from the time before the patient was born. Medical science does however, recognise that many diseases are hereditary in nature. This fact alone must mean that some diseases do stem from the time before the patient was born.

There have been numerous occasions where I have been told spiritually, that this is true, nevertheless, the doctors would not clinically ask if such an illness was hereditary. For example, when a child has been in the uterus, it may have been unwanted, unloved; its mother may have undergone a physical shock or the child may have even been parted too forcibly at birth. Such events can also attach themselves to the physical body of the child, via the mind or the body of the mother. This means that at some stage in the family-tree, the child has often suffered. Such diseases are the ones with hereditary tendencies. In such cases it is insufficient to direct the healing only to the mind itself.

The spiritual link to the physical body is known as the Silver Cord. It is analogous to the umbilical cord which physically links the child to its mother. When the umbilical cord is severed at birth, the child then begins life as an individual person or being. Similarly when the Silver Cord detaches itself from the physical body, the spirit detaches itself from the physical body. The body begins to decay, physical death occurs and the spiritual body moves on into the higher life; the real person or personality continues to exist.

It can be seen therefore, that many diseases can manifest themselves at the different stages in the soul's existence, even before physical life as we know it began. In my opinion, it is an absolute fact that in most cancer cases, the causes are often hidden in the mind or even deep in the subconscious mind. Lately, I have started to go with the flow of my own thoughts which arise from the intuitive diagnosis that I receive from Spirit. Sometimes I am momentarily directed to touch the Third Eye. I do not add any physical pressure with my fingers, I touch that point (in the middle of the forehead) for two to three seconds only. On touching that area, I visualise myself opening up an avenue into the subconscious mind, where often ugly thoughts or fears have been hidden for a considerable period of time. If we find that we are able to touch or spark off a thought in the patient's mind, we must encourage them to talk about it. We must bring those thoughts out into the open. This will help the patient considerably and will help unburden his or her deepest worries, fears, frustration and anxiety. But fear seems to me the most adverse condition, it is the prime cause in most cases. Fear attacks the emotional centres of the body. Invariably it attacks the throat. Our Spiritual Guides tell us that there is a very close relationship between the adrenal glands and the thyroid glands. Therefore, as we direct the healing energies in our mind, we must encourage new cells to be generated within the body. In addition, we must inject new thought-processes into the mind or the subconscious mind of the patient. This will enable them to restart and to rethink their mental attitude to life.

In recent times there has been an increase in the flow of cancer cases coming into the Sanctuary. In most instances I am dealing with them on the mind level. In every case I have noted a state of improvement in their outlook on life. In some cases it is fear of the unknown that is worrying them, or it could be fear of not having a true and loving relationship with husbands, wives, sisters or brothers. Any fear that interferes with the rhythmic pattern of harmony will produce cancerous cells, providing that that condition lasts long enough. Until such time that the mind has been able to change completely, in my opinion, the healers should continue to encourage patients to speak about fears and worries that deeply concern them. It is important for them to make these fears known and not to keep them hidden within those closets in their mind. In most cases, the Seventh Veil drops in the mind so that they can prevent other persons from knowing what is behind that veil. This veil has to be lifted so that we can ensure that harmonious conditions return to the mind, soul, and the physical body once again.

The day is fast coming when a closer liaison will be accomplished between Spiritual Healers and the medical profession. If this is not achieved, then it will result in Spiritual Healing finding its own level, which will be outside the range of the medical doctors. All knowledge must be exchanged in order that we can obtain the best results for those who are suffering.

I can remember one occasion, many years ago, when I was working in my little home, treating a patient one afternoon. Up to this point I had not been successful in helping this patient. I felt that the answer to this failure was not with me, after all I had been doing my very best, yet I was not getting the expected improvements that I was looking for. However, that one glorious afternoon, a wonderful opportunity arose whilst this patient was seated in front of me. Up until then, the atmosphere between us had been very harmonious. The Sanctuary door opened to allow another patient to enter the room. I did not know who this patient was, because I was deeply involved with the patient before me, in addition, I had my eyes closed. However, I knew instantly that the atmosphere had changed from one which was totally harmonious and spiritual in every sense of the word, to one which had become hideous, vile and brutal. I still pursued the thought of maintaining the harmonious conditions between the patient and myself, to the very best of my ability. I pursued this line of thought until the time of healing treatment had come to an end. When I opened my eyes, and even though no words were spoken, I witnessed a very ugly scene. I soon realised that the woman who had just entered the sanctuary whilst I was healing the person sitting before me, had recognised the patient. She was a sister of the person to whom I had just given healing. They had not spoken to each other for many years and they hated the sight of each other. Yet when the patient got up and faced her sister, the hatred between them seemed to magnify itself tenfold. Suddenly, before me appeared (clairvoyantly) a lady who stated to me that she was the mother of these two sisters, and that she was disgusted with the way in which they were behaving toward each other. She said to me that unless they settled their differences soon and made amends with each other, she would not be able to love or enjoy the companionship of either of them any more. I repeated to the sisters exactly what the mother had told me clairaudiently.

I said to them, "Did you love your mother?"

"Yes," said the first sister.

"Did you love your mother?"

"Yes," replied the second sister.

"Well you both have a funny way of showing it," I said. "Your mother has just been here before me and she says she is disgusted with the pair of you."

After I had spoken to both of them and reasoned with them, the situation changed, ending up with them embracing each other. They left the Sanctuary holding each other's hand. Within about six weeks of that day, both patients became healed.

Here surely lies the answer as to why both patients responded to the healing. Obviously one could have responded. However, they both responded simultaneously and I did not have to see them ever again. There was no need since the cause of the problem, the animosity and the hatred that lay between them, had been removed.

Another case which springs to mind, is that of a man who came to receive healing. He was out of harmony with himself, as well as hating other people. Other people also hated him. It resulted from something he had been told as a little child. In effect, he had been told that he was the ugly duckling of the family: "You are the one who has let the family down. You have also treated us abominably."

On questioning this patient in detail, I said to him, "Why should you hate yourself for that? Where is the spark of Divinity that is within you?

117

That which is within all of us?" I said. "God does not hate you, God created you," I continued. "Why have you alienated yourself from that Divine source that is within you?"

I could begin to realise how he felt about other people. But I could not fully understand why he had to hate himself.

Apparently, he used to look in the mirror every day and talk to his reflection. He would feed his reflection every day with his own negative thoughts. As a consequence, the whole bloodstream had become alienated. The whole tone of his body and his countenance was very poor indeed. He had become languid and was by now very slight in build. He was slowly but surely facing death. It was at this desperate point that he had come to receive spiritual healing.

I started healing him by first looking for the beauty, as opposed to the ugliness that was within and about him. I also encouraged him to think that it did not matter what other people said or thought, what was important was what he said or did.

"Do you still feel that you have alienated yourself from God?" I would ask. "Do you still go to a place of worship? Do you still feel there is something that is in harmony between you and your Maker? You still don't feel ugly then do you?"

"Yes," he said.

We played music, the type of music that he preferred. We began to obtain some harmony by listening to it. As a consequence, slowly but surely I was able to change his way of thinking. As a result, his countenance began to alter, his physical body began to change and improve. He began to look healthier and even began to look happy, albeit on isolated occasions at first. I encouraged him to meet people he became attracted to or felt friendly toward. I encouraged him to go to dancing classes and clubs and to present people with a smile whenever he met them. I told him it was important not to be seen to be sad or he would be a bore to people, who in turn would not like his company. In a matter of a few weeks he underwent a dynamic change. He became very much better and eventually left the Sanctuary. This was another true revelation to me and another example where it was important to get to grips with the causes of the illness.

I can also recall another event, when a mother brought her little child to see me. The child had been diagnosed by the medical profession as suffering from bronchial asthma. When I first saw the child, the skin lacked tone and colour and was very distressed because she was suffering greatly. I instantly felt that the cause of her illness had nothing to do with the physical body but lay somewhere else, where, I did not know. It felt to me that something was disturbing that child. Reflecting upon my thoughts, I saw a necklace made up of blue beads. In fact one blue bead stood out in my mind more than any of the others. I asked the mother:

"Have you ever had a necklace that has broken?"

"Why do you ask?" she said.

"Well," I said, "I felt as if a bead had been placed up the child's nostril."

"No," said the mother. In fact she denied it very strongly. She may not have known about it.

As far as I was concerned, that was the end of the story. Nevertheless, I still continued to see that blue bead in my mind. I became more and more confident that the cause of her illness had something to do with this blue bead, and sure enough, a few weeks later when the child had a coughing attack and also began to vomit, suddenly, out popped a blue bead. When the bead came out of the child's body, the mother instantly knew what I had been previously talking to her about. She removed the bead from the vomit, washed it, sterilised it and held it for safe keeping. These events reminded her of the fact that she had indeed owned a blue necklace and that it had broken. However, to this day, neither of us know how the bead got lodged in the child's nostril. We can only assume that somehow either the child or one of her little brothers or sisters had accidentally put it there. We will never know exactly. What we do know is that Spirit had discovered this fact and had been able to dislodge the bead. The story ended happily, the child never had another asthmatic attack.

Something operates beyond our normal range of understanding. How could I have diagnosed the presence of that bead in the child's nostril if the thought had not at first been planted in my mind? However, we must realise that we are working in God's domain. To me there is no other explanation. I am conscious of the fact that healers must never dismiss or limit the thoughts that come into their mind when they are healing. They must work upon these thoughts or images. Since it is these which are often the spur that will enable the healer to get to the true cause of the sickness which affects the patient.

Remember, if a healer is giving healing and there suddenly appears an object, any object or any thought which is outside their thoughts of healing, you can be sure that the thought or image is being transmitted from the Healing Guides. Very often such images are ignored. What a pity that this happens, because unfortunately it is the patient who is denied the benefit of the good health that would have been forthcoming. However, I am sure that as knowledge is developed and pursued, healers will be able to use these images and will eventually come to terms with their significance and reality. Here again I quote the words of Jesus who said, 'Marvel not at the things that I do, greater things than this ye shall do, because I go unto my father', which means that our knowledge of healing will continue to grow and grow, until such times as we will be able too do greater things than Jesus did. That I *do* believe.

Another incident that comes to mind very vividly was with regard to a young man who had feet which were so diseased that he could not stand. He could only stand on the outer sides of his feet, in a sideways-fashion. From the toes to the heels were large, open cracks, through which one could see deep into the soles of the feet; the arteries and veins. This young man was in such discomfort that he challenged me to even look at the condition of his feet. It was normal practice for me to treat the body fully-clothed, in this case, through the socks which he wore. I realised that when I touched his socks, his feet were heavily bandaged. Whilst I was healing his feet he threw down the gauntlet to me when he said, "If you only saw the state of my feet you would not touch them." From his remarks I knew instantly that there was fear in this young man's mind. So I said to him, "Take your socks off and let me have a look."

"I am warning you," he said.

"You threw down the gauntlet," I replied.

Eventually, I was able to persuade him to take his socks off and then remove the bandages. I knew that I had to break down that fear. I knew that I was not prepared for what I was about to see, but as the bandages were slowly being removed from his flesh, I was arming my mind for a shock and preparing for what I was having to face. On seeing his feet, it filled me with compassion. How on earth this man could bear to even stand on his feet was beyond comprehension. Literally, I felt so sorry for him that I would have kissed his feet. I could remember all the suffering that I had endured as a child, which in turn made me feel very sorry for him. As I placed my hands upon his feet, I was transported in thought to a graveside. I pursued that thought to the ultimate end, until the picture became very clear to me.

"Are you afraid of death?" I asked.

He said, "No." But I could see his body shudder as he reacted to the question. I realised that I had touched some 'button' in his mind. When I had re-bandaged his feet I asked him to put his socks back on. After looking at his feet I felt that I was able to get mentally closer to him. After some discussion, I learnt later, that one night, he and his brothers had been to a party. On their way they decided that they would take a short-cut home through a churchyard. Halfway through the churchyard his brothers decided to leave him there, and they continued without him. Little did they realise the damage that they would cause to this boy. As he began to run after them, he was approaching the tombstones and suddenly found himself standing on a grave. Although he was able to remove his hands from the headstone, he was not able to remove his feet from the ground. He was indeed petrified. When you consider that the hour was late and that darkness had enveloped him, he must have endured horrendous thoughts that arose from his imagination. His mind was consumed by the fear of the unknown and the fear that perhaps someone was around him. Eventually he decided to pick himself up from the ground and run away as fast as he could. He retraced his steps and found himself back on the main road again from where he could find his own way home. When he arrived home, the whole incident was just a big joke to his brothers. To him, however, it was far from a joke, since his feet had become powerfully affected by that fear which he had had to endure alone; fear of the earth, fear of whatever was under the earth; fear that he was standing on dead bodies. Such fears at so young an age took complete possession of his mind and in particular his feet.

I have never seen such a mess on anyone's feet. They appeared to have been cut and torn, with large crevices and cracks running down the central part of his soles. On close examination one could actually see the various tissues deep in the structure of his feet. One could actually see the arteries pulsating. To this day I have never seen feet in such a bad condition, and I sincerely hope I will not see such a condition again.

After we discussed the state of his feet and retraced the steps in his mind, I encouraged him to return to that night again. He then closed his eyes. I advised him to enter into the darkness and just to listen to my voice. I told him that the bodies that were once in that grave were there no more since they had long disintegrated into nothing: "Visualise yourself just standing on earth alone and realise that there is nothing physically wrong with your feet, but that their condition had resulted from the fear in your mind." And within a very short space of time, it was only a matter of a few weeks, I witnessed a perfect healing. As a consequence that young man was once again able to enjoy life.

Fear can result from all sorts of events. In these modern times, people are afraid of what is going to happen to them. What if they lose their jobs? What if they lose their homes? What will happen if they become a failure? People are afraid of public opinion. What people think of them. The images they create in their mind are very powerful and they become dogmatically negative in their thinking. As a consequence they live in an isolated, alien world of their own making. Others are not so well-off financially and feel inferior because they cannot clothe themselves or their children, with the same expensive clothes as those people around them. Healers must encourage all patients to love each other and put less emphasis on the material things of life. They must also learn to love life as it is presented to them.

It does not really matter what other people think, it is not important. You must encourage patients to think that they are very special to God themselves. They must learn to be contented with their own level of attainment or achievement in the world. It is healthy for them to aim for higher goals in life but in the interim period to be content with what they presently have, and try to find harmony in their minds and their surroundings. I can remember the time when I had to challenge myself because I was not what you would call a successful person. For example, I have never had enough money to possess a car. However, I was able to find happiness from within me, so I was able to tell myself that even though I did not own a car, I did own a barrow! With this barrow I was able to attend to my needs in the garden. It is a wonderful feeling not to be fearful of anybody or anything. Unfortunately there are different kinds of problems that from time to time confront us in life. Each step in life enables us to reach that next level of consciousness where we have to reason things out within our own limitations. We must learn that everyone is very special. We *all* have different gifts and abilities. We must learn to nurture and cultivate these gifts to the full and to try to radiate these feelings to others. We are all links in a human chain. We should learn to help everyone we meet in life, even animals. We must always strive for harmony and to try to come to terms with life's pattern. It is important that each and everyone of us is given the opportunity to achieve what we want to achieve. Yet there are times when we meet a stranger for the first time and we find we like that person instantly. Sometimes the complete opposite can happen; an instant disliking can occur. Why is this? It is because our spiritual beings project themselves on to the physical level of life. As a consequence our spiritual beings are not in harmony of thought. After all, we are two distinct personalities who do not harmonise. It is like Jesus said: 'You cannot put old wine into new bottles, or vice versa.' Similarly you cannot put an old patch on a new garment.

This line of thought makes me think of those wonderful surgeons who are able to transplant human organs. Despite their skill, sometimes the body rejects the work that they have done. I remember once being asked by Dr. Knutzen in Houston, Texas: "Could spiritual healing throw light on the fact that transplanted organs are rejected?" The answer I gave him, quite truthfully and simply was, that if the doctors were equally meticulous in matching the personalities of the patients as they are with matching blood and tissue types, they would achieve a far higher success rate. For example, take the case of patients A and B Patient A. may be the one who has passed on to the higher life, and it may be that his kidneys (or whatever) may be placed in another body. Patient A may have been a kind, generous, all-embracing type of person who never intentionally did any harm to anyone. If his kidney is being placed in the body of patient B, who was cruel, vindictive, spiteful, selfish and jealous to the core, there is no way that there could ever be any compatibility between the two tissue types. Therefore, a similar thing happens when two people meet each other for the first time. They recognise at a higher dimension something about each other that they do not like. This is the reason why they dislike each other and are not able to blend. Conversely, there are other people who you may meet for the first time yet you feel very content with them and feel as if you have known them all your life. In this case, you are on the same vibration of thought and you reverberate off each other. It is therefore very important to search for harmony and treasures of good thinking in order to preserve life. The Spiritual Doctors have informed us that a man or woman has to alter their thinking before they can guarantee their own well-being. Certainly, you can have an accident or injury that can harm your body. But if there are harmonious conditions prevailing in the mind, those damaged tissues will soon heal and become whole again. But if the mind is in disharmony, there is little hope of the tissues healing. Why? This should be a very important question in the mind of every healer. Why does this happen? Why is this? Why is that? Why doesn't this or that condition improve? Why is it that various ointments can be placed on damaged skin tissues and yet not produce any improvements? We must delve into the person's mind and find out why. Why is it that there is some kind of disharmony between the mind and the various body tissues? It may be due to a physical body in the form of disease or lack of natural healing. The healer may be able to transmit new thoughts into the patient's mind and pray for good influences to come into his life. One must recognise the whole healing process and the way in which it works. It begins with the mind and follows on to the blood, the nerves and the glands. For example, if the patient is suffering from a skin disorder such as eczema, the healing must first be concentrated on the mind, which in turn will stimulate the blood and then the nerves, which then stimulate the sebaceous glands to produce the necessary lubricating fluids for the skin tissues which will ultimately produce the physical healing. When such communication has been successful, one will soon see the skin taking on a new tone of good health.

At this stage I would also like to mention epilepsy. One must recognise that epilepsy can be very strongly influenced by the environment that is about us. In particular I am referring to the electromagnetic stream that flows through the body. This stream can be strongly affected by the mind. When tension rises in the mind, the electromagnetic stream can increase substantially. It can reach such a level that it can take complete control over the physical body. This power eventually builds up in a similar way that energy builds up in the atmosphere, where it takes a huge electrical storm to release. Such events are followed by calmness, freshness, and the sun shines once again. Likewise, the electromagnetic stream in the body breaks down and an enormous electrical explosion takes place in the brain. But what causes this stream to build up and why does it not disperse itself in the normal manner through the physical body? Normally there are vents in the body which permit the energy to ebb and flow, thus preventing a build-up of surplus energy in the body. If such a flow of energy is prevented from venting, it builds up and must eventually be released. This explosion occurs in the brain, resulting in a severe epileptic attack. I have been very much aware of epilepsy. I have witnessed the effects of both grand and petit mal attacks. In such epileptic cases, one must first aim to restore serenity to the mind and bring balance to the electromagnetic stream flowing through the body. All this is done through the process of thought. In all cases involving epilepsy, if spiritual healing is directed correctly, harmony is restored to the body and the epileptic condition is completely cured.

I hope these words of explanation have been of some use to someone, somewhere who may be reading this book. I wish you well and my love goes out to you all in your time of need and times of stress. I also send out strong thoughts of love and healing to the doctors who work diligently for the benefit of mankind, for the alleviation of pain and suffering. My thoughts also go out to the nurses who tend to the needs of the sick and help cure all forms of illness and disease. God's love and blessings be with you all.

These words have been my words of explanation of Spiritual Healing. Always remember that we can all be humble channels for the Divine Healing Power of our Almighty God.

Chapter Nine

MEDIUMSHIP

In my opinion, mediumship is a planned act, it is not a planned act of the medium, but of Spirit or God. If you have been chosen to travel along the path of a medium or you have chosen this pathway yourself, you must never, never dictate the terms of your mediumship. You must let these gifts unfold naturally, you cannot say you will be a clairvoyant, clairaudient, or a healer.

In the early days of my mediumship I already knew that I could 'see' and 'hear' things that most other people could not. I experienced these things as a little girl, however, I did not know anything about trance mediumship or healing. As I progressed through life I certaintly learned that the medium is continually tried and tested. Every medium that I have ever heard of, from the times of Scripture up to the present day, has been tested in some way. They are tested for their strength, their endurance, their truthfulness, their loyalty, their very substance is tested. Throughout the ages mediums have suffered tremendously at the hands of others, often enduring torturous conditions. In comparison with the early mediums, my life has been relatively easy. Today, things have changed and conditions for the mediums are much less difficult. Nevertheless, today's mediums still undergo various trials and tests of their faith. It is necessary that they are tested before being entrusted with the true energies and the gifts of the Spirit.

My entry into mediumship was so lovely and joyous. Events happened so quickly that I could not see beyond the immediate joy and happiness I was experiencing. Sometime later I began to realise that events were going against me. I knew what it was to suffer emotionally, for I had been married, then suffered the indignity of a divorce. It must be realised that at the time, divorce was very much frowned upon by society. I also knew what it was like to endure degredation and deprivation. After my divorce I was left destitute, and this experience was very traumatic as I suffered very deeply emotionally. Although it was very upsetting, I learned from it. This made me become even more involved in my work, and I decided to throw in my lot with Spirit. Later, I found myself being mocked by most people. I was a source of social ridicule wherever I went. Some people became very hostile towards me and very brutal and hurtful with their verbal accusations. Life became almost unbearable. I thought that at one time I would have to throw in the towel and accept defeat. Fortunately, I decided to stick with my task and I learned to become stronger as I fought more and more battles. I found that from being strong, I furnished myself with a tremendous armoury of will. I had the will to win and fight for what I knew to be right and true. This brought with it a sense of tremendous determination and resoluteness. It gave me the right to do what I wanted to do with my life. I told myself that I had as much right to do this work as any other person in the world. They had no right in stopping me from doing what God wanted me to do, and through all these struggles I found myself growing spiritually taller.

One day in 1971, I was on my way to the local shops when I stopped and chatted to some friends for a while. Instinctively I said, "I am sorry, I have to go now."

"But you have only just arrived," replied one of my friends.

As I prepared to leave, one of my friends accompanied me to the top of the street. As we started to cross to the other side of the road, a car stopped and a man got out and enquired: "Excuse me ladies, could I have a word with you please? Could you direct me to the Temple of Light Sanctuary please?"

"This is the person you are looking for," replied my friend, indicating me.

When we arrived at the Sanctuary he explained that his name was Mr. Morgan and that he lived in Prestatyn. He had just lost his only child, Eluned, at the young age of twenty-one. She meant everything in the world to him and his wife. I could see by his expression that he was still grief-stricken. We had tea together and then I prepared for my evening healing work. After I had finished my healing session, he left and returned home. During his brief stay with me he had sufficient time to relate to me the amazing story about the death of his daughter Eluned.

Eluned had suddenly been stricken with acute appendicitis, which resulted in hospitalisation and emergency surgery. She recovered quite quickly, but two days after the operation she informed her father:

"Let's do as much as we can together, for I am not coming out of this hospital alive!"

Her father replied anxiously, "I know you have had an operation, but you are not in a serious condition. Appendicitis is a common complaint and you have had only a minor operation."

Nevertheless, Eluned insisted that she would shortly die. Her father remained confused and worried, for he could not really understand her remarks. To put his own mind at ease he asked to speak to the doctor so that he could obtain his professional opinion. The doctor explained to him that the operation had gone well and that there had not been any complications. He assured the father that Eluned would be well.

When Mr. Morgan and his wife visited Eluned again the following day, Eluned explained to her parents that the doctor had visited her to reassure her that all was fine. The doctor also warned her not to upset her parents. She replied to the doctor by saying, "I am not going out of this hospital alive!"

On the Friday night, her parents visited her again and took Eluned's clothes with them in readiness for her discharge the following morning. During conversation Eluned again told her parents that she would not leave the hospital alive, saying, "You can take me home dad, but to be honest with you, you will be taking me home dead!" This distressed her parents very much. After visiting, they left her in bed and all seemed well, but in the middle of the night they were called to the hospital again. Eluned died at 2.00 a.m., and just before she died she told her father to come and see me. The doctor in charge of Eluned was astounded at her death. A post mortem was carried out and although her operation had been successful, examination revealed something that the doctor had never seen before. He said that her heart was very small; equivalent in size to that of a very old lady of about ninety. He had never seen a human heart that was so small. In fact he was amazed that she had lived to twenty-one years of age.

In July, after Eluned's death, Mr. Morgan invited me to visit his headmaster, Mr. Spencer, in Prestatyn. Mr. Spencer was losing his eyesight. When I met Mr. Spencer, he invited me to join his spiritual friends. I soon realised that it was a highly spiritual group of people. I could also sense that physical phenomena would take place. Neither Mr. Spencer, his wife, nor his group of friends, knew what was going to happen. I did not mention my feelings to anyone. I first gave Mr.

Spencer some spiritual healing. A short service followed with nothing special happening. Later I was invited into another room for some refreshments. I felt the atmosphere getting colder, which was a clear sign to me that the Spirit people were drawing closer. I then realised that I had left my handbag in the room in which I had just given Mr. Spencer healing. As I re-entered the room to retrieve my handbag, I noticed that Mrs. Spencer was in the process of closing the curtains. She turned to me and said, "We will try to give you a nice gift tonight. We are sitting for physical phenomena."

"I know," I replied.

"How did you know?" enquired Mrs. Spencer.

"I could sense the cold etheric condition in the room when I was giving healing to Mr. Spencer. This is a sure sign to me that physical phenomena will take place. During healing, I generally only experience the generation of heat or a pleasant warm condition, I explained."

Mrs. Spencer continued the conversation by explaining to me that their medium was a Direct Voice Medium. "We hope our Guide will be able to come and talk to you," she added. This made me feel very happy and I realised that this was indeed a great privilege. After Mrs. Spencer had finished preparing the room, we were all invited in to sit in the darkness. As I re-entered the room for the second time, I noticed a silver star on the table. We commenced the 'Circle' with a prayer, and after a while I found myself speaking quite casually with the medium. Suddenly, the room was transformed from total darkness into the brightest white light that I had ever seen. I looked around and saw that all the original members of the 'Circle' were still in their seats and checked that no lights had been switched on. I soon realised that the light was emanating from the silver star that was moving about the room. Just as suddenly, the voice of the Guide spoke. He said that his name was Abraham. As he spoke the star was floating beside me.

"Marian," said the Guide. "It is no chance that you are here in Prestatyn. Eluned is also here and she sends her love to you. You will go to my country and speak there on behalf of my world. You will take the Christ-energy there. In two years time you will find yourself addressing my people in my homeland."

"I am sure that I will not be there," I replied politely. "I have no intention of going there at all. I could not fly there, for I am terrified of flying."

129

In October, some months later in the same year, I found myself reading the *Spiritual Healer, a* magazine in which it was reported that the National Federation of Spiritual Healers was going to make its first pilgrimage to Israel. This immediately reminded me of what Abraham had told me some months earlier. Within about half an hour of reading the article I had decided to overcome my fear of flying and fly with them to Israel. I talked over my decision with my niece Gwenda and asked her if she wanted to join me. She agreed that she would. Sometime later I found myself speaking to my brother Ewart and said to him, "Are you coming to Israel with us?"

"No!" replied Ewart, "although going to Israel would be one of life's treasures. I could not afford to go with you."

Nevertheless, I knew in my heart that somehow Ewart would eventually join us.

In the meantime Gwenda and I continued to save for our trip which was planned for the 12th of May, 1973. Around the Christmas of 1972, Ewart's father-in law passed away. During the family get-together it was mentioned that Gwenda and I were going to Israel in the following May. In the course of conversation I quite casually said, "Don't forget that Ewart will be coming with us. Ewart of course was very annoyed, for he had already made it clear to me several times that he could not afford to go. Then around April, 1973, I received an unexpected phone call from a friend, Ruth Anderson, informing me that her husband Gilbert, the tour organiser, had had an accident and would be unable to make the trip to Israel. Since I was the oldest Healer of the tour party, it was subsequently agreed that I should become tour organiser, which in turn would entitle me to a free trip. The money that I saved for the trip then became available to Ewart. He was going to make the trip after all! This pleased my Aunt Bess very much, for she felt safer if Ewart was by my side to look after me.

When I saw Ewart some days later, I said to him, "I was right, you *are* going to Israel after all."

"You know that I can't possibly afford to go," he replied.

"Oh yes you can, you have a free trip."

Ewart looked at me in disbelief, but eventually agreed to join us.

To be equally honest, I also doubted that I would ever give a public address in Israel. But I did. I gave an address in Jerusalem, Tel Aviv and also in Tiberius. Naturally, every day that we were in Israel I prayed for strength so that we could work effectively as a team of healers. The conditions in Israel made this difficult to achieve for there was always intense heat and humidity.

Prior to one of the healing sessions in Jerusalem, it was on a Tuesday, the dark clouds began to form and soon it poured with rain for several hours, enabling us to give our healing demonstration in, what was to us, ideal, cool conditions. The following day, Wednesday, we were at Tel Aviv, again the conditions were hot and humid. But at 3.30 p.m. the dark clouds formed again, the wind rose and it again poured with rain! As soon as the healing session stopped, the rain stopped and the weather returned to normal. During the next seven days we did not encounter any rain at all. On Thursday the following week, just before we were about to give another healing demonstration, the clouds formed and the wind increased, and once again it rained.

Our stay in Israel was not always an easy one for we often found ourselves in discussion with the Rabbi who of course was not in agreement with our work. Nevertheless, Abraham was true to his word.

During a later visit to Israel in 1984, I went to Emmaus, just outside Jerusalem, to visit the wonderful shrine where Our Lord and Saviour appeared to Simon and Cleopas. I had sustained a slight injury to my foot and therefore it incapacitated me and prevented me to a great degree from following other members of the group. So I went quietly and sat under a tree outside the shrine. I found myself linking in with the beauty of the surroundings and the sacredness of that place, for it is still in its original unaltered state. Whilst I sat there quietly meditating and seeking to attune with the powers of healing, my old friend Harry Edwards appeared before me and spoke at great length. I had a wonderful time with him because he gave me so much joy and happiness at the reunion. He wanted me to convey to Ray and Joan Branch who currently run the Harry Edwards Sanctuary, at Burrows Lea, Shere near Guilford in Surrey, his loving thoughts and to state quite clearly that he will never use anybody else other than Ray and Joan. He would come to them, he would guide them, and help them, but that his whole attention, or at least ninety-nine percent of his attention, would be in his Sanctuary in Burrows Lea, for that is the light of the world in this country (U.K.) – and is the part of the world in which I live.

It was as an indirect result of meeting Gordon Turner that I met Harry Edwards! It was many years ago, and we were thinking of ideas by which we could generate extra money for the building fund for our future church. As a consequence we invited Mr. Gordon Turner who was

Chairman of the National Federation of Spiritual Healers to give an address in the local Miners' Welfare Hall at Ystradgynlais. At the end of the meeting we had a Healing Service and Gordon Turner worked with us. When I returned home he said to me, "I have witnessed your work and it is beyond reproach, so as Chairman of the N.F.S.H., I am going to recommend your application to join the N.F.S.H., if you wish to do so. (My application was accepted in 1957.) Sometime later I went to one of the N.F.S.H. schools and it was there that I first met Harry Edwards. Without appearing to boast, we 'gelled' immediately together. He spoke to me at length on many occasions and I explained to him how my work was being rejected by some members of society. He told me, "Go forth and be a warrior for Spirit like I have been." From that time, I became a great admirer of Harry Edwards and I had the privilege of training with him on a few occasions. He was truly a great man who literally put Spiritual Healing on the map and was instrumental in getting Spiritual Healing legally accepted in the U.K.

I was also privileged to attend Harry Edwards' eightieth birthday celebration which coincided with the twenty-first anniversary of the N.F.S.H.

I have always held Harry Edwards in the highest esteem, and I remember one time when there was a gathering in London, when Harry Edwards and I were talking with some people and somebody asked him " . . . but what sort of person are you really Mr. Edwards?"

"I will leave Marian to answer that," he replied.

I said, "Harry Edwards? Harry Edwards is the Rolls Royce of all Healers!"

I will always remember the loving and guiding thoughts that Harry Edwards sent out to us. I know no greater thing than that the Sanctuary at Burrows Lea has been left in the careful, kind and loving care of Ray and Joan Branch.

I am sometimes asked if I can tell if a person is ready to pass on into the Higher Life. The answer is yes, but I am not always privileged to obtain this information. Very often I get the impression that there is an ebbing and flowing of the life-force from the body and also feel that a person will not live very long. I can clearly remember one such occasion when I was asked to visit an old lady who was ninety-years of age. Prior to my visit I had been told that she had worked as a linguist and could speak nine languages. When I entered her flat, I had the shock of my life! She had a frail, little body and did not have any legs. During the Second

World War she worked in an embassy in Czechoslovakia as an interpreter, mainly translating the replies of interrogated prisoners. One day she found herself translating the answers of a male prisoner who was well known to her. Naturally she did not want him to suffer, so during the interrogation she deliberately translated his answers incorrectly. The Nazi interrogators eventually discovered this, and as a result, amputated one of her legs.

During her imprisonment she had to make several journeys between prison camps, aided by a single crutch. On one of these journeys, her group was captured by the advancing Russian Army. During her capture the Russians learned from one of the other prisoners that she was an interpreter and as a consequence she was forced to work for them. In time they discovered how she had lost her leg. As fate turned out, another prisoner came before her one day and she tried to protect him also. The Russians discovered this and in retribution they told her that they would do what the Germans had done to her, and this led to her second leg being amputated.

As I sat down beside her, I said, "Hello my dear how are you?"

"I am so glad to see you. Will you pray for me?" she asked. "Please pray out loud so that I can hear you. Please ask God to take me. I am tired and I want to go home."

"Of course," I replied.

In prayer, I made her needs known. In preparation for my visit she had already put the kettle on so that she could make me a cup of tea. When I heard the kettle boil I said, "There is no need for you to make a cup of tea for me, let me make it."

"Oh let me make it, it may be my last act of kindness on earth."

As it happened, she did not pass on at that time. Later, I was asked to visit again. As I sat beside her on this occasion she said, "It did not work did it?"

I tried to make light of these remarks by saying, "I don't think that they have got your home ready yet, they must be spring-cleaning it."

She asked me to pray for her again and I did so. When I left, I later found out that by the time I had reached the end of the street where she lived, she had died. This was one particular occasion where I was not privileged to know that the death was imminent. But as a general rule, I suppose I am aware of this approximately seventy-five to eighty percent of the time. If I am asked to help someone on their way, I do it, but I never dictate the terms, I always ask God what to do. I always begin the prayer by making the person's request known to God. After all, He knoweth best.

Similarly, I don't force healing on anyone, in fact it is a personal rule that I don't help anyone unless the person is humble enough to ask for it. I never dictate the terms of healing. Sometimes I have overheard a conversation where a healer has said to someone who is ill: "I think that you can benefit from Absent Healing, put your name down on the Absent Healing Book." I think such actions are wrong. You can inform the person that Contact Healing or Absent Healing is available, but you cannot force healing upon them, otherwise you interfere with that person's free will, which in my opinion is wrong. Equally, the sick person must ask for healing, they must not be allowed to take the work of God for granted. This would be wrong. I feel very strongly that the healing energies that flow from God are too precious to be used in this way.

I also do not prescribe any form of medicine for my patients. Firstly, it is illegal to do so, and secondly, as a Spiritual Healer, I am not qualified to do so. For the same reasons, I do not permit the sale of any such 'remedies' in our church.

Sometimes I am asked how I help someone who is suffering because of 'Karmic debt'. In my opinion such persons cannot be helped until that debt has been repaid; they will not be cured until they are prepared to accept their past misdemeanours, and put their own house in order. In such cases, I advise patients that I am there to help them spiritually in any way that I can. I always ask them if they recognise that they have done anything wrong. Often the person will express sorrow and remorse for whatever past misdemeanour he or she has done. However such statements in themelves do not repay Karmic debt. The only way this can be repaid is by actually doing something. Words alone have no effect. The person has to do something positive to recompense for the wrongdoing or the injustice that has been done. Both thought and action have to take place. Often I do not know what debt has to be repaid, and in such cases, many actions may have to take place; they may even have to continue after physical death.

During one of my visits to Austria I was taken by my friend, Dr. Marian Mentel, an historian, to see a lady who lived near the Austrian/German border. This lady was suffering from Multiple Sclerosis. As we entered into the room where the lady was sitting, Dr. Mentel said, "Elizabeth, I have brought Marian to see you and to help you."

"Marian can never help me," replied Elizabeth. "This is my Karmic debt that I have to repay and I am not ready to reconcile myself with it yet."

This case illustrates that Elizabeth obviously recognised her own condition but either would not or could not reconcile herself with God. In such a case, there was nothing that I could do to effect a cure. Elizabeth was insistent that she could not be cured, for she reasoned that her Karmic debt was too great for her to repay.

In contrast with Elizabeth's case, I have had a patient who visited me for fourteen years, and in my opinion she was physically cured. One day I politely said to her, "I think you are better now, you can stop coming to see me now if you like."

"Do I have to stop?" she replied.

From her reply I realised that her soul still wanted fellowship, and she continued to come to see me. Her visits were like Communion to her. She said she still needed the visits, just as I needed my daily diet of food.

Her situation always serves to remind me that each case must be treated individually.

As a trance medium, I am very close to the Spirit World, in particular, I am very close to my Door-keeper, Raheede, and my main Healing Guide, Dr. Clive Osborne. The knowledge in the Spirit World is vast and the following paragraphs serve to illustrate its diversity. For example this is what Dr. Osborne had to say about A.I.D.S.:

"A.I.D.S, is caused by an imbalance of the sexual desires of man. A.I.D.S. is not a new disease, it goes back a very long, long, time. In days gone by, in particular, in the days of the Romans, they used to carry out the most hideous and vile acts with regard to sex. Sex would take place between father and daughter, sister and brother, sometimes even after death had occurred. Some would have intercourse even when the body was in a state of rigor mortis. Of course such acts were vile and unnatural. A similar unnaturalness prevails today. God created male and female, both are complementary to each other. Disharmony sets in when man disobeys the natural laws that govern him. In the case of homosexuality, a mixing of the cellular substance of the body takes place during intercourse, which are alien to each other. In turn, this can generate new forms of bacteria or viruses in the body, which can become deadly. The natural law is that only male and female should join together and this is the case in both the animal and plant kingdoms. When a person has become infected by A.I.D.S., the disease can also be transmitted to others by blood transfusions. Even innocent people can therefore become affected.

A.I.D.S. in on the increase throughout all the nations of the world. The only way that it can be stopped is by guidance and the return to natural law. In lesser developed countries, birth-control will have to be introduced, in order to reduce the occurrence of A.I.D.S., which in some countries is already at epidemic levels. If birth-control does not take place, a whole nation of affected species will arise."

He also talks about the effects of drugs and alcohol, and the human aura: 'There are also those people who abuse themselves with alcohol and drugs, they leave themselves open to the Spirits on the lower Astral Planes. These Spirits can have an adverse effect on people and often try to influence the continuence of alcohol or drugs. As with all kinds of illness or disease, unless the person's mind is prepared to alter its thinking, a cure cannot be effected. The mind is always the driving force towards the overcoming of sickness. The mind affects the endocrine glands and the body's ability to heal itself. Everyone is subject to the effect of the positive and negative thinking that takes place in the mind. To effect a change, it is essential to think deeply and positively, but it is not easy. But it is very easy to be negative.

'Many people today, including some healers, 'speak of the Etheric Body and also of the human Aura. The Etheric Body is the non-physical counterpart of the physical body and it can be visualised as the space that exists within the atomic structure. The Aura is the energy field that exists around the physical body. Many psychically gifted people can see the Aura in its many different colours. In 1908, Dr. Kilner developed chemical screens, which when looked through, enabled the human eye to see the auric energy field. Similarly, Kirlian Photography enables a manifestation of the auric field to be photographed when high frequency electricity is used.

'I mention the Etheric Body and the Etheric Energy Fields because many people think that disease can manifest itself in the Aura. Many mention that the illness is caused by the Aura. This is not true. The Etheric Energy Field is only a reflection of the physical body. When there is a change in the physical, emotional or mental states, this will reflect itself in the Aura. However, the Aura does not cause the physical body to become ill or diseased.'

I have found trance mediumship to be helpful in many diverse ways. It can assist on the physical, emotional, and the spiritual level. For example, here is Raheede's answer to a person who, in January, 1993, asked about the political future in the U.K:

"There are going to be political changes but not as it is patterned at the moment. A new party will be formed which will link with one which is already in being. This new party of a few members (SDP) is going to link up with the old party of many years ago (Liberals). They will link together and will be able to change the shape of things. Your country is not going to the 'left', as you say. You will not go to the 'right', as you say, but you are going to be in the centre. I also envisage that there is going to be a time of great famine in the world. There is also going to be much unemployment, not only in your country (U.K.), but in many other countries as well. I also told you this many years ago, and as I told you then, it will force people to stop and think. Because of man's lust for power and because of man's greed for wealth, man can destroy himself through greed. Man must learn to give. That is the motto that should be in operation. That is also the motto of the Great White Spirit who you call God. He gives into life. The angel forces give into life. The whole universe gives, but man, the higher species, only draws to himself. Man wants more and more; the more he gets the worse things become. You will find that as man works less hours he will receive more wages, eventually you will be paid for doing nothing. That is not good. In your Scriptures it states quite emphatically that . . . 'By the sweat of thy brow thou shalt eat bread.' Likewise man must create. Nothing comes from nothing. Both the worker and the manager want as much as they can, they want everything. They don't care who sinks while they sail. There will come a time when they are going to be challenged. What are things going to be like? They will either have to slow down, or continue and eventually come to a standstill. In the end this will result in a worse deal for everyone. There will have to be intelligent thinking that is able to bring about a balance. That which the third world countries produce cheaper will be bought by the western world. The same western people who are crying out for more wages. They are only pricing themselves out of work. This does not really make sense does it? We say it would be better for both the managers and the workers to have less wages and be content in their work. A man who does not use his energies will use them in other ways, for example, vandalism. Years ago, the men of your world used to go to work and work very long hours and when they came home at the end of the day, there would often be cross words between the mother and her sons, who were the wage earners. The arguments would arise because the mother would want her sons to wash before they ate their meals. On the other hand, the sons had used their energies in strenuous work and looked forward to relax, sleep and recharge their physical bodies and nervous systems. Today, although there is a lesser amount of physical work, and modern technology, sometimes the robots are treated better than your own body. In order for you to progress, man must learn from his mistakes and to use his energies that the Great White Spirit has given to him. Having used his energies correctly, he will not have the inclination to fight with others or to vandalise.

"Although man has done a tremendous amount in the technological world, he has also gone backwards thirty to forty steps. Man should utilise his thinking to help those who will suffer famine in years to come. Man will have to start thinking about the basic necessities of life that are required for the physical body. There will always be a need for that.

"There is also a great problem being generated in your world today. Man produces so much rubbish, including plastics, etc., but he cannot find sufficient space to dump it. He therefore produces piles of dangerous substances which can produce sickness in the bodies of many people. Nuclear waste is another problem. There is also the waste produced in the vivisection laboratories. Your scientists want to make tests on poor animals, so that he can prove that their actions are for the ultimate good of mankind. What they are doing is morally, fundamentally, and spiritually, evil. They are making a mockery of the Creation. What does this work prove? It does not prove anything. What they are doing is pure evil. After the poor animal has been drugged, and eventually dies, it is thrown onto the mother earth and pollutes it. You also graze cattle on the same soil which in turn produces milk for human consumption. The whole logic is wrong. Man is getting too far advanced, but in the wrong direction. Man will have to stop and pursue the avenues that are more advantageous to human life."

These short accounts of some of the true experiences in my life and some of the teachings of Spirit serve to illustrate the wisdom of the Spirit World.

Today, I still find myself being tried and tested by Spirit. However, the testing is not so frequent and not so demanding anymore. Unfortunately, I still have some enemies and some still live close to me. But the day will come when they will alter their thinking, either in this world or in the next. No matter what they think, I will always offer them all happiness and blessing in their lives. One thing I am certain of, they will never, never experience all the love and happiness that I experienced in my life, as I work in my Church with those whom I care for.

Animals too experience the same kind of love. They realise that love is easily understood.

I have many friends in the animal kingdom including cats, dogs, horses, cows, bulls, and sheep. I have treated all kinds of animals in my life. However, I can remember one specific instance, on a Good Friday, when a little lamb was brought to me by a farmer's wife who had a farm in Sennybridge. It had a tumour on its brain, and it was continuously bleating its little heart out. After I gave the lamb the 'Laying on of Hands' it stopped bleating and became very peaceful. I later learnt that the lamb remained peaceful for the rest of the day but in the evening it quietly passed away. This occasion brought to my mind the words of Scripture which say: ' . . . to behold the lamb of God.'

I shall never forget that Good Friday. Everything in my life appertaining to mediumship has been very, very special to me and has been vital to my spiritual growth. I only hope that the rest of the days of my life will continue in this way and that I shall be able to continue to share these treasures with others.

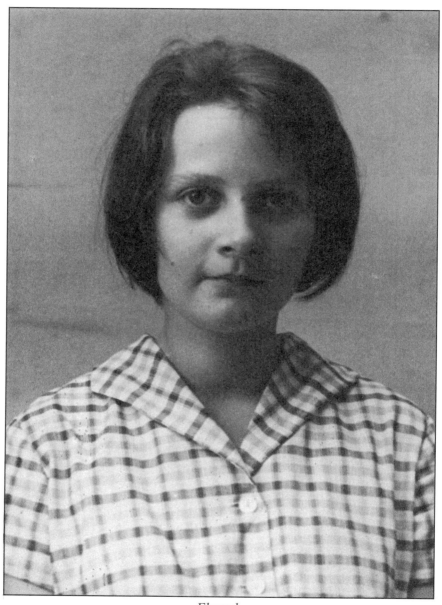

Eluned.

Chapter Ten

SPECIAL CASES

Even though one must examine and treat all cases of sickness individually, there is nevertheless a general law that governs all cases. No case is healed by chance, the healing energy is always intelligently directed by the Healing Guides. Before a healing can take place, the true cause of the illness or disharmony must first be understood. Some cases can take far longer to heal than others. Some can take but a few seconds or minutes to effect a cure. Others may take a far longer time. In most cases however, the healing is progressive and may take several weeks before a cure is effected. Most patients find some form of benefit or upliftment in the first few weeks. When they tell me this, I know that I am on the right track. In some cases it my take several months or even years before a complete healing takes place. Those who are cured sometimes continue with Spiritual Healing because it affords them continuing fellowship or spiritual comfort.

When it takes a long time to effect a cure, in general, the patients have undergone some very traumatic experience during their lives. It may even have been when the patient was in the mother's womb, or it may be a condition inherited from previous generations, or it may even have been in a past life. Such conditions act as a block, preventing or inhibiting the healing energy. In my experience, it is not always possible to bring about a complete cure, but in all cases, the patient is always helped to a greater or lesser degree. The examples which will be cited in this chapter, show the diverse nature of Spiritual Healing. These cases also serve to illustrate that the human intelligence alone could not resolve them. I certainly was not capable of resolving them on my own, I know that I do not have the necessary intelligence, after all, I spent most my schooldays on the bed of sickness. The unique nature of these cases proves that the healing or knowledge that is responsible for the cure, comes from a higher level of intelligence. To me, it proves that the healing intelligence comes from a Divine source which is from God. This knowledge is utilised by the Spiritual Healing Guides who in turn use the physical minds and bodies of certain gifted people, mediums or healers, to channel or transmit this healing intelligence to the patient.

I can recall the case of Susan Hackett. Susan first came to me as a little girl of about two to three years of age. When I first saw her, I had never seen, what seemed to me, such a hopeless, pathetic case. Susan had no neck, her head just seemed to sit directly on her shoulders. Nevertheless, a miracle did unfold before my eyes. It must have been a miracle, for there was no way that I had the intelligence to cure her. Of course, there must have been some form of cervical vertebrae present in order to hold her head on to her shoulders in the first place. But there was definitely no visible evidence of a neck.

After healing Susan for several months, she was eventually called into hospital in London for surgery. Even though similar operations had been carried out there before, none had been successful. In fact Susan was the only case to be cured. Susan's parents were only told of the risks involved the night before the operation took place. The surgeon probably did not want to worry them unduly for too long a period. Susan's parents telephoned me at about 11.30 p.m. on the night prior to the operation. They were naturally very worried and distressed. The doctor had told them that although he would do his very best to help Susan, he was quite frank when he told her parents that he had not had success with similar cases. The operation did turn out to be successful and Susan's case was mentioned in both the *Spiritual Healer* magazine and also in the medical journal, the *Lancet.*

In Susan's case, it took the combined efforts of the medical profession and Spiritual Healing, and many years to effect a cure. Today, Susan is a very beautiful, intelligent young woman who is studying to become a lawyer.

In another case, a young boy of about four years was brought to see me. He had no fingers on either hand, he only had tiny stumps of gristle where his thumbs should normally be. In the truest sense, he did not have any hands. The doctor had prepared his mother for the fact that they would most likely carry out an amputation of the wrists so that artificial limbs could be fitted in readiness for when he started school. When his mother first brought him to me, he was very agitated and aggressive and would not sit still long enough for me even to touch him. He used to say to me, "I don't want anything to do with you, I want to go home." I would reply to him by saying, "Go if you like, I am not stopping you!" Sometime later, I began to realise that I was not making progress with him, so I decided to use some basic psychology.

Whenever he came to see me, he invariably wore a beautiful sweater. One day I remarked to him how beautiful his sweater was and that I would like to knit a similar one for my nephew Lyn. I winked at his mother as I said to him, "Oh! you do look very smart today." Then I turned to his mother and asked, "Do you have the pattern for the sweater, so that I could borrow it?"

She turned to me and also winked as she replied, "No!"

"Well, how am I going to knit a similar sweater for my nephew Lyn who is not very well?"

"Oh, I have an idea," I said as I turned to the little boy. "Would you let me count the rows and stitches on your sweater?"

To my delight he let me count the rows and stitches. I had at last made contact with him. As I approached his wrists, I took a very long time counting the fine stitches around the cuffs, allowing more time for the healing energy to flow. After that first contact, slowly but surely, progress was made. The bones began to grow, at first in the form of tiny stumps of gristle. These then grew more elongated to form fingers. Eventually, I can honestly say, his hands grew to become almost perfect. The only feature that was defective on his hands, was the nail on his little finger which did not grow fully to its normal length. Over a period of about eight months his hands were almost perfectly formed, in time for him to start primary school.

In another remarkable case, a little baby was brought to me by her mother. She was carried into my Sanctuary in a small carry cot. She was a beautiful little child and her pretty face remains quite clear to me even today.

I remarked to the mother how pretty the baby was.

"Yes," replied the mother, "but she is no better than a cabbage, Miss Butler."

"She is not a cabbage, in the eyes of God," I replied.

"How old do you think she is?" asked the mother.

"It's hard to tell," I said, "perhaps ten or eleven months old!"

"She is twenty-one years old," replied the mother.

She added later that the little girl only had half a brain.

I can't find the words that would truly express my astonishment. I said to myself, "What could I do?" I knew that I alone could do absolutely nothing, nothing at all.

I placed my hands on the small child in perfect love and I surrendered her completely to God. From that moment, slowly but surely, she began to grow. Over a period of several months, her brain first began to develop. Her little hands became stronger and firmer. Some months later, she first entered the Sanctuary, walking unaided. She slowly and steadily continued to grow. She progressed so well that her parents found private tuition for her and after many years she became fully developed. She eventually got married, and today that same little child has three children of her own. I wish I could meet that young woman today. Even for me, all this did not seem possible when we first met. Today my faith is so strong that I believe that anything is possible and no one will ever deny me the power of the Holy Spirit.

During the period when I was visiting different states in America, I found myself in a small town in Massachusetts. During that time, Spiritual Healing was not legalised in the U.S.A. While I was in Massachusetts I was asked if I would visit a teenage girl of about seventeen years, at her home. I cannot remember the name of the girl but do remember that there were two doctors present when I visited her at her bedside, and that she was in a curled-up position, unable to move any of her limbs. She had been in such a condition for about ten years, since she was about seven years old. As I knelt down to approach her lying in the bed, I instantly sensed that I wanted to withdraw from her. As I drew nearer to her I felt more repulsed, I did not know why, I sensed that she was someone that I did not want to be close to. It was not that I did not want to help her, it was more like a feeling of not wanting to touch her or be near to her.

As these thoughts raced through my mind, I could not understand why I was being alienated by her presence. As my mind tussled with these very strong impressions, I slowly became aware of what was causing the condition of the child. I turned to the doctors and said, "I am going to talk to her now. If I am on the right track you can expect some kind of reaction from her. You may not like what you see, but please be tolerant and bear with me." The doctors nodded in agreement, but neither they nor I bargained for what was to happen next.

"Are you afraid of death?" I said to the young girl. With those words, her whole body seemed to shake and I could sense that she was afraid.

"No! I am not," replied the girl.

"Yes you are," I said.

As the conversation slowly progressed, I began to visualise the body of an old lady in a coffin. I had not seen the old lady before, but the Guide told me that she was the grandmother of the girl on the bed before me. As I talked to the girl, it became apparent that about ten years previously her mother had lifted her up to kiss her grandmother who was in her coffin. The child was extremely frightened and was pulling away from the coffin. Of course these were the impressions that I had sensed when I first approached the girl. So I said to the young woman, "You were afraid of your grandmother weren't you?"

Instantly she began to scream, "I don't want to talk about it!"

"But you must talk about it," I replied.

"Do you want to be like this for the rest of your life? You must talk about it. Speak up, speak up!" I demanded.

She continued to scream and scream. I sensed that the doctors present thought that things had gone far enough and that they wanted me to stop. Slowly, the screams began to subside, dying down into loud cries, then into gentle sobs. She then reached for a tissue to wipe her eyes. Up to that point she had never been able to use her hands, her body had remained almost totally rigid.

"Look," I said to her, "you are moving your hand!"

"Can you move your wrist?" I asked.

"Yes," she replied.

"Can you move your arm?"

"Yes," she again replied.

Events progressed from there, with her bending her elbow and raising her arm above her head. At the sight of this, the doctors became quite amazed. Before I left her home she could stand and was able to take a few steps. Previous to this, she had endured almost ten years of total paralysis.

On another occasion, a mother brought her married daughter to see me. The daughter was in a very distressed state of depression. Her condition was so acute that she could hardly relax at all. This was affecting all aspects of her life. She was afraid of life, for it was just meaningless to her. Her mind and body were full of shock and fear. From talking to her mother, I discovered that at the age of eight or nine years, the daughter had complained of severe pains in the region of the middle ear. Her mother took her to see the local general practitioner, who in turn referred her to an ear, nose and throat specialist, who failed to diagnose anything organically wrong with the girl. He deduced that the girl was faking her illness so that she could avoid attending school.

A few days after visiting the specialist, a large swelling began to develop around her cheek-bone. This made the parents realise that the girl's illness had not been a fantasy. They visited the local general practitioner again, who once more referred them to the same specialist. He then began to treat her by giving her an injection in her face. Unfortunately the needle broke, leaving a substantial portion still imbedded in her face. This traumatic event naturally left the girl with a tremendous amount of shock in her body and an equally tremendous amount of fear in her mind, leaving her in a highly nervous, tensed state for the rest of her life.

I soon realised that this was not the full extent of the girl's condition, when the girl's mother mentioned to me that she wanted her daughter to get well so that they could both visit the mother's sister in Canada. These words caused the already nervous condition of her daughter to become even more acute. This suggested to me that something else had to be revealed before a cure could be expected. Because the daughter was in such a distressed state, I demanded that the mother should speak up and reveal the total picture to me.

As I questioned the mother, I could sense that the girl did not want her mother to reply. However, before the mother could reply, the daughter interjected, "I don't want my mother to have the needle."

The child of course was referring to the inoculation that would be necessary for them to have before a visit to Canada. The thought of another injection was compounding the disturbed state that already existed in her mind. She had visions of the needle breaking again. I soon realised that it was this fear that was the main cause of her illness. She was petrified that either she or her mother would experience the needle breaking again. Within about six to eight weeks of this first discussion, she was cured. This event again reinforced the fact that before a healing can take place the true cause of the condition must first be removed.

On another occasion, a lady came to see me who was a health visitor. She asked me if I was prepared to visit her home and give healing to her nephew, who was a young man of about thirty years of age. She informed me that during the Second World War he had been interned in a

Japanese prisoner of war camp. Naturally I went to her home, which eventually resulted in me having to visit the man for about four hours every week over a period of several months. He had not spoken to anyone for years, not even to his own parents. He used to spend hours of each day locked away in the horrors of his mind. During these many months, I could not get close enough to him even to lay my hands on him. Eventually I decided to sit down on a chair and look at him, to try and make eye contact with him. Even this was extremely difficult, for he would stand in the opposite corner of the room for up to three hours. His hands would always be at the side of his body, always extremely straight, as if he was standing to attention. His fingers were always pointed downwards, consequently, on either side of his body were two puddles of liquid formed from the perspiration that ran down his arms. Very often two dishes would be placed on the floor to contain the volume.

As he stood there transfixed, I used to say very quietly to him, "Talk to me! Tell me what is going through your mind?"

As I recall that occasion, I can still see that man very clearly in my mind as he turned his head to look at me so, so strangely, yet his eyes projected the horrors of the grotesque scenes that he had had to endure. Eventually he allowed me into his mind and explained to me just some of the things that he had been forced to witness. He had been impelled to watch the hands of his fellow soldiers being tied behind their backs, and then forced to kneel in front of him, where he was witness to their beheading with a sword. Such was the mental torture that he had to endure. Consequently his mind was full of fear and he was unable to speak of the horrors that he had witnessed.

After his camp was liberated, he was accompanied by medical officers to Cardiff railway station to be met by his parents. At that stage his parents were not prepared for what they saw, for their son's condition had not been explained to them. At first, they did not recognise their son, such was the severity of the state that he was in.

After months of these four hour, weekly sessions, I said something to him, I cannot recall what I had said, but it triggered off something in his mind which must have reminded him of those scenes of horror.

I can see the look on his face as he turned his head to look at me. It seemed as if he could murder me.

"Excuse me," he said very quietly, "I must go and wash my hands!"

Those were his first words. I will never forget them. By washing his hands he was symbolically trying to wash away the horrific scenes that were still in his mind.

From that day he progressed and I was able to encourage him to sit on a stool before me and let me place my hands upon him. At first he did not like this for he was still very afraid. After much patient encouragement, he continued to progress. The periods when he was standing in the corner with his hands dripping became progressively shorter, and the periods of giving him healing became progressively longer. When I arrived one day, he made me my first cup of tea, which I deemed to be a great privilege indeed. Although this was but a simple, humble gesture, it said to me that he was beginning to repay my kindness and that at last he was returning to a state of normality. As soon as he became well enough, one of the first things that he did was to go and watch a football match. I have since lost contact with this man, but in the mid 1980s I was told that he had become successful in business.

After witnessing such dramatic cures, which to me were truly miraculous, I decided that I needed to understand something about how the mind and body functioned. Consequently, I decided to participate in one of the study courses organised by Harry Edwards. Each night before I went to sleep, I used to set aside one hour for study. One night, I was sitting up in bed with *Bailiere's Book of Anatomy and Physiology* in front of me. As I became deeply engrossed in this book, I slowly became aware that the atmosphere in the bedroom was changing, it became cold and I sensed a spiritual presence there. This spirit-being spoke to me and said that she wanted me to write to her son who was working as a judge in Uganda, who was in serious danger. I was told to write the letter in the Welsh language, so that anyone who opened it would probably not understand it. She did not give me her son's address, however, I promised her faithfully that I would do exactly what she had asked of me.

As I went shopping the next morning, the first person I met was the sister-in-law of the judge. I asked her for her brother-in-law's address in Uganda. At first she was extremely reluctant to give it to me. I did not know why this should be so. I explained to her what had happened the night before. She still would not give his address to me but she was prepared to pass the message on to him. I told her that I could not do that since I had promised to write and send the letter myself. Sometime later, she telephoned me saying that she was prepared to give me his address provided that I destroyed it after I had written the letter. I promised her that I would do that, and that is exactly what I did.

I later established that the judge had received my letter about eight days after I had posted it. After reading the letter he immediately went to speak to his superior and asked permission to leave as soon as possible, since he had just received some disturbing news from his home. His superior agreed to this provided he could get a fellow judge to deputise for him. After making such arrangements, he immediately left and caught the first ship for Southampton at around midnight that same night.

On his return home to South Wales he established that all the judges in that region of Uganda were *massacred*. Later, he presented me with a hand-carved ivory statuette of the Madonna. Since the statuette was carved in Africa, the facial features of the Madonna are naturally those of the African race. After that sad event, the judge never returned to work in Uganda again.

The telephone in my home is almost continuously in use, with many people asking for help for their friends or loved ones who are desperate for help. It is very difficult, if not impossible, to console such people within a few minutes, invariably such conversations can last for half an hour or even longer. Consequently, I often get complaints from others, for they have not been able to get in contact with me by telephone. However, after I have explained the situation to them, most people realise the position that I am in. On one occasion, I received a telephone call from a Mrs. Down asking me if I would be prepared to help her son Royston. Some days later, she brought her handsome young son to me. After discussing the situation with both Royston and his mother, I discovered that Royston suffered from epilepsy. Although I never saw him when he had an attack, such was the severity of his attacks that he was capable of turning over and breaking the desks of his classroom. This indicated to me the he suffered from 'grand mal' epileptic attacks.

During this period, there was a friend of the Down's family who was working as a secretary for Harry Edwards. Since I was treating Royston, I received a letter from Harry Edwards asking me about Royston's condition. Whenever Royston would have one of his violent attacks at home, his parents would invariably telephone me. Often the telephone calls occurred on a Saturday, coinciding with the time when we sat for spiritual development. One Saturday evening, the parents were so distressed that they asked me to see Royston. Although I agreed to their request, I explained to them that I could only see Royston before our sitting. Fearing the fact that Royston could have an attack at any time, I explained that I could not allow them to take part in the circle.

On their car journeys to see me, Royston would invariably start to cry. He would receive healing from me, yet on the way home again, he would have another epileptic attack. This was a very unusual experience for me, as most patients, after they have received healing, achieved a state of betterment. In Royston's case, it was the reverse. Although Royston was not mentally ill in any way, these events made me realise that there was something affecting his mental condition. After I had given him healing, later that Saturday evening, I asked Raheede what was wrong with Royston and how I could best direct the healing. The fact that Harry Edwards also wanted to know about Royston seemed to add extra urgency to this question. To my surprise, Raheede advised me to tell Royston's parents to bring him to our sitting on the following Saturday. During this sitting, Mr. and Mrs. Oliver Grey, who were close friends of my aunt, were also present. They had travelled from Coventry to visit my aunt, after being on a recent holiday to Greece. Whilst on holiday they became aquainted with a very nice Greek gentleman who could speak some English.

During the sitting Raheede explained that the Greek gentleman was spiritually present in our circle that evening, for he had only recently passed away, not long after the return to the U.K of Mr. and Mrs. Grey. At that period of my life, my mediumship was capable of physical phenomena. The Greek gentleman's face partially materialised during our sitting. Naturally this put the fear of God into Royston's young mind. Almost immediately he wanted to leave the circle. Raheede prevented him from doing so, for Raheede realised that he was afraid of the fact that certain aspects about him may be revealed to others who were present. Eventually the circle drew to a close and Royston and his parents left. Sometime later I received another telephone call from Royston's parents explaining that he did not want anything more to do with me or my circle. I said that I understood why this was the case. I explained to them that the house in which they lived was on the site of an ancient Roman burial ground. Most of the bodies that had been buried there were those of epileptics, and their souls were feeding off Royston's physical body. His parents naturally could not believe this and could not accept the fact that their lovely home was on the site of a Roman burial ground. Some years later it was established that within the vicinity of their home, many Roman artefacts had been found, but it was never confirmed that their house was actually on the site.

Whether those who read this book believe this true story or not is irrelevant to me. However, I later passed on this information to Harry Edwards, and being the great master healer that he was, he dealt with the matter. His efforts were able to release the souls of those Roman soldiers into the Spirit World. About one month later, Royston was found to be free of any further epileptic attacks. Normally patients who are so severely affected by epilepsy cannot be expected to live very long, since their bodies cannot sustain the continuous strain. However, when I contacted Royston in March, 1993 to ask permission to include his case history in this book, he told me that he was forty-six years of age, happily married, with a family of his own. He is still quite well, however, he does take medication and does sometimes suffer from slight losses of memory, and confusion.

Just prior to the opening of our church in 1987, Royston and his father presented me with a beautiful wooden cross. Today that cross hangs proudly on our altar, in honour of God, who healed him.

I can also recall a case involving a Mrs. Harper, who was a doctor's wife of French nationality, living in Potardawe. One day she brought her elderly aunt of eighty-two years to see me. Her aunt could not speak a word of English and I could not speak a word of French. Mrs. Harper said to me that she would leave her aunt with me and whilst I gave give her aunt healing, she would utilise the opportunity to do some shopping. At this time, healing sessions took place in the Sanctuary of my home. In front of where the patients sat to receive healing, was a small altar which I still have today. At the base of the altar was a small vase of flowers, above which hung a small cross and a picture of Christ.

This elderly lady was totally blind, unable to distinguish night from day. Just before I gave her healing, I commenced the healing session by playing Beethoven's *Moonlight Sonata* on the record player. As is well known, Beethoven was stone deaf. As I placed my hands over the lady's eyes, my hands became sticky. It was as if my fingers had been dipped in some form of glue. If I tried to move my hands away from her eyes this sensation of stickiness was even more profound. At the same time, I could actually feel her eyes opening and closing. A few seconds later, I heard the old lady say, "Christos, Christos." I asked her what she was trying to explain. She replied by repeating the same words, "Christos, Christos." I soon realised that she could see the picture of Christ hanging on the altar in front of her. I was truly amazed. As I turned to look at her, I could see some liquid running from her eyes and down the sides of her face. I soon realised that whatever that substance was, it must have been acting as a barrier, like some kind of curtain preventing her from seeing.

I left the Sanctuary to get a flannel to wipe her eyes and face. After wiping her eyes she said, "Maria, Maria, Maria." I soon realised that she was looking at the ivory statuette of the Madonna, previously given to me by the judge. When her niece returned, the lady immediately spoke to her in French. They were both bubbling with excitement. I was equally excited trying to explain events in English! Despite the language barrier we all quickly and fully understood what had happened.

Mrs. Harper also had a sister named Mrs. Louis Valleaux, who lived in Liège in Belgium. She had married a Belgium gentleman who had been in a concentration camp during the Second World War. Mrs. Valleaux trained with me for several months, eventually returning to Belgium to carry on her own work there.

When I first met Louis she could only manage to speak through a small aperture at the side of her mouth. Invariably she held her hand in front of her mouth as she spoke.

One day I said to Louis, "Why are you hiding your face like that?"

"Because I have cancer of the tongue," replied Louis.

"Let me have a look at your tongue," I said.

"No!" she firmly replied.

"Please let me see it," I continued to ask on several occasions, but the answer was always no. Although she allowed me to place my hands on her face, she never opened her mouth.

I later discovered that Louis had had about half of her tongue removed during surgery.

One day I was attending a birthday party at Mrs. Harper's home at which Louis was present. I became determined that somehow or other I would use this occasion to put my hands on Louis' tongue. In advance, I prepared myself by giving my hands a thorough washing. As I approached Louis I asked a question, I cannot remember exactly what the question was, but I can clearly remember that as she opened her mouth to reply, I stuck my fingers inside her mouth and gently but firmly grabbed hold of her tongue. At the same time I begged her to open her mouth so that I could see the condition of her tongue. At first she was reluctant to do so. But on persisting, she opened it. Without revealing the horror of what I saw, I could understand why she had always kept her mouth closed. Her tongue was black! She agreed to let me hold her tongue between my thumb and index finger. Within a matter of a few weeks, the remaining portion of her tongue returned to its normal healthy pink colour, and not only that, but it grew to its full size.

I have since lost contact with Louis but I hope that one day we will meet again.

During the Second World War my brother Ewart was in the British Eighth Army. One day his wife said to me, "I have not heard from Ewart for a very long time. I do hope that he is safe and well." In reply I said that by using the pendulum we could try to find out. So I dowsed the map of Africa, but there was no response with the pendulum at all. My sister-in-law naturally became quite anxious for she thought that Ewart had been killed. I reassured her by saying that Ewart could have been posted elsewhere. As I moved the pendulum away from the North African coast, it began to gyrate. As the pendulum approached the Sicilian coast, it began to gyrate even more strongly. This told me that I was getting closer to where Ewart was posted. As the pendulum approached the Italian coast, an even stronger reaction took place, becoming most pronounced at a place called "Bari".

I have found the pendulum to be a very accurate instrument, especially if used in the correct way with the right intention of purpose. I have used this method of Radiesthesia on many occasions for many, many diverse problems. However, I cannot stress too strongly that it should never be used as a game or plaything, it must always be used sincerely. In turn I have found it to give me much help, strength and guidance. When it is used in this way, I have always found it to come up with the correct answers. Like Water-divining, I consider it to be a very precious, natural gift from God.

After using this method, within a few weeks, my sister-in-law received a letter written in Welsh, to avoid the scrutiny of censorship. In the letter, Ewart explained that he was stationed in the same place as his brother-in-law who lived in Barry, South Wales. This confirmed to both of us that the pendulum had correctly located Ewart, even though he had been stationed hundreds of miles away.

I have sometimes been asked by the police to assist in finding missing persons. Unfortunately, I have not always been successful. However, there was a case of a young boy who had been missing from a welfare home in Brecon. The police contacted me to see if I could assist them in locating the boy. I explained to them that I could quite clearly see that he was located near a viaduct and that his body was trapped under a river bank or ledge. The body had become entrapped during a flood. I was not able to be more specific than that. The police informed me that they had dragged the river area and had not found a body. Sometime later there was another flood and the boy's enlarged body was released and later discovered floating in the river.

Although I have endured most kinds of suffering in my life, I have also enjoyed much happiness; the joy of helping to ease pain and suffering, and the joy of helping to resolve major problems, and the happiness in helping to locate missing persons. Such joy cannot be fully explained in words and no price can ever be put on it. Only those who have helped others in a similar way can begin to understand that joy, and the love of God that I feel. One really has to experience that special kind of joy which occurs when that wonderfully dynamic energy flows from the mind through the hands and into the body of a patient. You realise that you are touching on some spark of Divinity, some finite state of being that must be experienced in order to be fully appreciated. It makes one feel so jubilant and elated that one wants to share such experiences with others. Of course, that was how the word of God was spread in the first place.

I would also like to pay tribute to my colleagues who have assisted me and worked alongside me over the years. I will always be thankful for the help given to me by my niece, the Rev. Gwenda Jones. We have worked together almost from the beginning. Mr. John V. Bowen has also worked with me for twenty-seven years. I first met John when he came to me for help those many years ago. During our association, I soon realised that he too had the healing gift, and he has turned out to be a very fine healer. Life is never easy and whenever the chips were down, Gwenda and John were always there to share the burden. It will make me feel very proud when Gwenda becomes elected to the Presidency of the World Federation of Healing, in 1995.

I also wish to recognise the services of Desmond (Des) Bennett and Oswald (Ossie) West, alas, both have passed on into the Higher Life. In more recent years there has been Barry and Doreen Howell, Carolyn and Wayne Jones, they too have done so much in helping to carry the spiritual load. People often forget that I too have to endure personal difficulties, after all, we are all human-beings. My grateful thanks go also to our Church President, John Thorne, and his wife Helen. Thanks too, go to Margaret Taylor and Margaret James who have served on the Church Committee for many years. We also have trainee healers in the pipeline such as Claire Cole, Shirley Howells and Eirwen Harvey. It has also given me great pleasure to witness the very good healing work that Mr. Lyonel Thomas of Penarth has done. He is currently the Secretary General of the World Federation of Healing. It was when the church was first formed in the Sanctuary in my aunt's home that I discovered and informed him of his healing gift. Our friendship has since stood the test of aeons of time. In addition to his healing work he has done a tremendous amount of excellent work with the people. There are numerous charities that have benefited from the fund-raising work that he has achieved with his band of young people. They will all ensure that the work will go on into the future. There are many, many others to whom I am eternally grateful; it is almost impossible to mention every one individually.

Despite the efforts of everyone, none of us can yet fully appreciate the meaning or purpose of life, or the pain that others may have to endure in this so-called modern world in which we live. Nevertheless, we can reach out to help them in various ways. It may even be through meditation, the "Laying on of Hands", through traditional medical science, or even by the simple intelligent use of music or Colour Therapy. Modern scientific man is only beginning to realise the benefits of such complementary therapies. We cannot yet truly evaluate the depths of this knowledge, which is starting to find its own level. We are beginning to realise that we are only touching the fringes of the dynamic energies than are around and about us. When we fully understand these energies, I am sure that man will be able to utilise them to overcome all forms of malady that exist in our world.

My greatest personal joy thus far in my physical life has been my ability to communicate with my Spirit Guides. They are able to inform me with precision, the true causes of disease. I hope that some of the cases cited in this chapter have been able to convince the reader of this. I am totally convinced that the healings that take place are not due to me personally. Yes, I am an important instrument or channel, but I can assure you that the knowledge used to effect a cure could not have come from me. Whenever the true cause is established, an improvement in the health state always results. Always remember that before a perfect healing can take place the causes must first be removed. This is a simple fundamental law that must never be forgotten by any Healer.

When I receive such information from the Spirit Guides and I inform the patient what I have been told, at first, and in most cases, the patient cannot remember or appreciate the significance of the information given.

Quite often the cause of the present condition may have manifested from an accident or an emotional disturbance many years previously. Invariably, after the patient has discussed or corroborated the information with a friend, only then is the patient able to fully appreciate the significance of the information given to him. Raheede, who is my beloved Friend and Spiritual Door-keeper, is but one of about two hundred Guides who utilise me. When they were on the Earth Plane, they came from all walks of life; humble Carpenters, Nurses, Doctors, Scientists, Lawyers, etc. It is a complete misconception to think that all Spiritual Guides are Red American Indians, Ancient Egyptians, or Chinese.

My main healing Guide is Dr. Clive Osborne, an English medical doctor who originally lived in Essex. Dr. Osborne is almost permanently with me and is able to implant impressions upon my mind as to what is happening in the body of the patient. Dr. Osborne, often in conjunction with Raheede, is usually able to inform me how the condition came about in the first place. Another of my main Healing Guides is Dr. John Peters who was a Paediatrician and naturally assists with children. I am not always in direct, perfect communication with him, but he is able to communicate with me through Dr. Clive Osborne. I am also assisted and guided by Dr. Graham Moffat, and Dr. Karl Hoffman, who was an Austrian cancer specialist. In the very early days of my mediumship, Edith Cavell sometimes used me. She was a nurse who was shot at dawn by the German forces in October, 1915, the year that I was born. In the early days she could communicate with me directly, but today this is a very rare occurrence. In more recent years the Guides have informed me how to take 'short cuts' and how to best direct the healing.

I also feel that the Healing movement is progressing in its own right. One must realise that in the U.K. in particular, waiting-lists to receive traditional medicine are getting longer and at the same time the numbers that can afford private treatment are decreasing. This will allow Spiritual Healing and other complementary treatments to come more to the fore. In our church, none of our Healers ever get paid for their Spiritual Healing work, however, we always welcome free-will donations for the upkeep of the church. God, however, does place a charge on his work; it is not a financial one, but He does expect people to put back into life something in return for His work. He certainly expects that they should have a better understanding of the suffering of others or render service to others less fortunate than themselves. No matter how the reader may evaluate Spiritual Healing, I can from personal experience only rate it first class, second to none. Jesus of course was the Great Master Healer of our time. He was able to heal mentally (by faith) and through the 'Laying on of Hands' (by touch). The more that man is able to realise this, the more spiritual progress he will make.

I would also like to mention those people who think that they can progress through life without God. Sadly, they are truly deluding themselves. In the course of my own life I have met many atheists or agnostics. They have come to me and in their own despair have tried to find God, but do not know how. I have never turned them away from God. I think that during their hour of need it is essential that they are helped. Conversely the clergy often make a similar mistake when they ask why it is necessary to have Guides to assist in healing. Why do you need Indian or Chinese Guides? In such instances I quote the Scriptures to them where it is written: 'Tarry ye in Jerusalem until the Comforter shall come and he shall teach thee many things.'

"Who do you think these Comforters are?" is my reply to them when such questions are asked. Unquestionably they are the Angels of God who guide us and help us through the pathway of life. Through the wisdom of God's power they are there for us. They guide us to think rightly. I have already stated earlier that the Guides are not always of the Indian, Egyptian or Chinese races. I also have to remind people that Jesus was not a European man, he was a Eastern man. Invariably the Eastern races worshipped a God that they had never seen. What is God? God is Spirit.

In my opinion there is no disease that will fail to respond to Spiritual Healing to some degree or other. Spiritual Healers are often ridiculed and we are sometimes accused of deluding ourselves. Those who make such accusations have either not experienced Spiritual Healing or are ignorant of its true potential. The classic example of this is when someone says to me: "You think you did your best for so and so but he died!" That is classically one of man's greatest misunderstandings of our work. This makes me very annoyed, for no one has the right to deny the work of God. In most cases He has done all that is spiritually and practically possible to help them. Where He has not been able to cure them, they are then promoted into the Higher Life, which is the final destiny of us all.

The Ivory Madonna.
Presented to me by the Judge for saving his life.

Chapter Eleven

CANCER

During my life I have given hundreds of trance addresses, however, most of these have been given to private groups and individuals. Consequently, the content of such an address is invariably a private matter which should never be discussed with others and never, never written about. On a few occasions I have given public trance addresses where the Guides who use me are able to talk to the people. They in turn can listen to what the Guides have to say and are given the opportunity to ask questions. Unfortunately, few of these public trance addresses have been recorded. However, in August, 1992 I arranged to give a public demonstration on trance mediumship at the Temple of Light Church, where one of my Guides, Dr. Clive Osborne, talked about cancer. The following is a verbatim transcript of what Dr. Clive Osborne had to say about cancer:

"Cancer is not a new disease nor is it a disease even of the last century. Cancer has existed even before the days of the Nazarene , or the Christ existed on the Earth Plane. As is recorded in the Scriptures, He was able to deal with cancer in those days. The lady with the issue of blood was cured by touching the hem of His divine garment. This unfortunate lady was suffering from cancer of the uterus or the womb. In those days there were no such treatments as chemotherapy or radiotherapy. Nevertheless, you must recognise the tremendous, wonderful healing power that the Nazarene had. That lady knew that it would only be sufficient for her to touch the hem of His garment for her to be healed. If you accept this to be fact you will have to go all the way with me, so that you can understand how such a power can effect the physical body. She was instantly healed by the power of the mind. She knew that by utilising her mental energies she could be cured simply by touching the hem of His garment, and was able to benefit from the vast reservoir of energy that emanated from his body.

"Today, we are becoming very familiar with this disease called cancer. We are getting to understand the root-causes of the trouble. I say to you, that invariably, all causes of cancer are of a psychosomatic nature, that is, the trouble originates from wrong thinking and wrong living. The mind becomes powerfully affected by the negativity in life. It can be caused through fear, frustration, anxiety or an inability to express a particular path or achievement that you want in life. You may want to aspire to great heights which you may not be able or capable of achieving. Consequently you overburden your body with the forces which are destructive to the physical body.

In the first instance it is the mind that is affected. From the mind the blood and the nerves become affected. The brain is the physical counterpart of the mind. Wrong thinking in the mind upsets the physical structures of the brain and lowers the general tone of the circulatory systems. This in turn causes a cessation of the normal flow of harmony to the physical body.

"I want you to reflect very deeply upon what I have said, especially those of you who wish to aspire to become Healers. You must first understand how the body functions. If you have a problem such as fear or a frustration, then you must face up to it and deal with it, otherwise, it will affect the physical body. I want you to look upon your body as you look upon your car. The sympathetic nervous system in the body can be compared with the accelerating system in your car. Similarly the parasympathetic system in your body can be compared with the braking system. There is a continuous interplay between the sympathetic and the parasympathetic nervous systems in the body, i.e. a continuous interplay between acceleration and braking. If you are able to educate the mind sufficiently, cancer is not allowed to take place. Let us assume that you are going on a journey. Let us also assume that you are perfectly healthy, but events do not proceed in the manner that you want them to go. You start thinking wrongly and you permit anything of an upsetting nature to enter into your mind. This will result in the thyroid gland coming under attack. The thyroid glands are very powerful emotional centres in the body. When shock or fear is injected into these glands, through the mind, they become non-functional to some degree. Then the serious trouble begins, because you have taken the first step in preventing that flow of energy that is vitally essential to the formation of the red corpuscles in the blood, which are manufactured in the bone marrow. The red corpuscles become deficient in iron.

"I also want you to realise that the thyroid glands, and the adrenal glands which are located above your kidneys, are very closely related to each other. The adrenal glands are effectively the central-heating system of the body. So as your adrenal glands become affected you not only become deficient in adrenaline and thyroxin but your whole blood supply begins to lose its strength. So as the blood is manufactured and circulates in the various limbs of your body, you do not have the correct texture in your blood for your well-being. Once such a condition has taken hold of the body, it is not so easy for the body to become healthy again. You may become hospitalised and you may even be given chemotherapy or radiotherapy. As you realise, you cannot give chemotherapy or radiotherapy to the mind! When you go to hospital for the physical body to be healed, it also necessitates that the mind must also be healed. If this is achieved then you can begin to reverse the order.

"As Healing Channels, you can attune yourselves to whatever Healing Guides that come to work with you. Give the Guides the opportunity of doing their best for the patient, by aspiring to reach the minds of the patients. Since in most cases the disease is of a psychosomatic nature. Therefore, you must seek for good influences to reach the mind so as to correct incorrect thinking, anxiety, or to overcome fearsome conditions. If through years of practice, you recognise that there is a lack of thyroxin in the body, then you must aim to release the brake that is preventing the thyroid glands from functioning. You must look to stimulate the sympathetic nervous system. You should seek for good influences to release the brake, i.e. you must reverse the thought process, so that the thyroids can become functional again. As the thyroids begin to function you will notice that the body will take on a new, healthier tone.

"When you have what is known as 'secondaries' in cancer, you can reverse this process all the way, until you have reached the epidermis region in the skin. Until you have worked through the whole process from the mind right through to the epidermis, there is always the possibility that the cancer can recur again. You must always follow this thought process right through to the end.

"The spleen is situated under the left-hand side of the ribcage. What is the function of the spleen? The spleen's function is similar to that of a factory where used blood is reprocessed. The blood, which in the first

161

instance was created in the bone marrow, travels through the body doing all that is necessary to ensure correct functioning of the body. The age of blood can vary, it can last between three to eight weeks. Those people whose blood lasts seven to eight weeks do not use a lot of strength or vitality at work, invariably they take life very easily. In fact they lead sedentary lives, they only do those things in life that they have to do, or do that which pleases them. Their blood will last much longer when compared with a person who has to work hard at daily tasks. For example, a mother who cares for her family and also has to hold down a job, who is constantly on the move, is utilising more of this blood energy. Now what happens to this blood after it has done its job? It has to be disposed of, in which case it is channelled to the spleen where it is reconverted into what are known as leucocytes. These leucocytes are the scavengers in the body, which can multiply by the millions in the bloodstream. They devour bacteria which may be lodging in the bloodstream of the various arteries and capillary networks. These leucocytes are therefore continually dealing with such bacteria and its disposal.

Now if you suffer from cancer, invariably, it might necessitate a blood transfusion to increase the platelet level in the blood, so that your body can function correctly. An over-abundance of leucocytes being produced by the spleen not only destroys bacteria but destroys the platelets as well. This in turn necessitates that the patient has to continually go back to the hospital to have more blood transfusions. So what has happened to the spleen to cause this? Illogical thinking of the mind causes a disharmony in the organ and instead of having a balance between the sympathetic and the parasympathetic nervous systems, i.e. the bodies stop/go system, the sympathetic system is over stimulated, producing more and more leucocytes so you have to apply the energy that comes through from my world to restore this balance. So that when you reduce production of leucocytes you will find that the platelets that you have been given via a blood transfusion at the hospital, are allowed to function,

"Many diseases, which may also be cancerous, are produced in an unborn child. When that child comes into the earth life it can be riddled with cancerous cells. You can work on the child as much as you like but you must work through the Healing Intelligence which is there from the Supreme. Through the Healing Intelligence, the Healer is given the wisdom to understand. You must not only work upon the child but you must also work upon the mother or even the grandmother, since the disease can be inherited from the parent or grandparent. Therefore you must work on the mind of the child, the mind of the mother and even the grandmother's mind. Now this only deals with the mind, but the Healer must also be intelligent enough to adapt himself to deal with the physical body. If the heart is defective, you must place your hands on the heart. Similarly if the tonsils are infected, you must place your hands on the throat. But where do you place you hands when the disease may have originated two or three generations back? You must place your hand on the baby's navel, for that is the point where the mother and the baby were attached to each other, so that the Healer must work on both the mental and the physical levels. This information comes from the Healing Intelligence and permits the Healer to obtain that information which enables him or her to get at the root-cause of the disease, the Healer must also aspire to understand the body and its functions. Many people treat their motor cars better than they treat their bodies. That I can assure you. This is often done through wrong thinking and wrong living. Where does wrong living fit into this overall scene? Many people, for example, are constantly poisoning their bodily systems by over-indulgence with sugar. Sugar is lethal! Sugar is stored in the liver for such times as you go for hours without food. Specific substances are released into the body to enable you to carry on with your normal work. But if you over indulge in eating sugar you will set up a condition of disharmony within that organ, because the liver will eventually not be able to cope with the excessive sugar levels. The time will be reached when the liver itself will not be able to cope.

"You must always be intelligent when dealing with cancer. Even though the Spirit Healers actually carry out the healing, if the Healer and patient can also adopt correct thinking then so much more can be achieved. It is no good just to say that the patient has a bad head and therefore ask for healing to be directed to the head. The Healer has to find out more than this simple fact. Aspire to find out more and let knowledge grow. The Great White Spirit (God), as Raheede always said, 'It is He who created the body in the first place.' It is He who created the body's intelligence system. You must therefore act intelligently, think intelligently and behave intelligently. You must also learn to respect the body and ask the body for forgiveness if you have over indulged. You may laugh me to scorn for having made such a statement, that is your privilege. Nevertheless, what I have told you is quite true. You must have respect for your body and ask for forgiveness for breaking the natural law. That natural law which governs and controls your physical body.

"Many, many people, as they have come over to my world, have asked: 'I do not want to come over to your world yet. I have a lot to do for my family at home.' But they are given the opportunity of learning the true mechanism of the intelligent force that governs us all. Then they have to come back to work through Healing Channels to help those that they have left behind.

"Cancer can be healed. I don't care what type of cancer it is, be it a tumour on the brain, a tumour in the digestive system, skin cancer, or leukaemia, etc. I don't care what form the cancer is. It can be healed even in a short space of time. If you utilise the forces intelligently that govern you, so that you can bring control back to its basic needs and desires, thereby restoring harmony. We are dealing a great deal with cancer in this church, and no doubt, in future, many hundreds and thousands will come for treatment. As a result we are experiencing many more cures, since knowledge is beginning to seep through in abundance. This knowledge is transmitted to our earth channels who in turn can reflect that knowledge on to the minds and bodies of the patients. Do not be afraid of cancer in the physical body. But certainly be afraid of cancer of the soul! There is no cure for cancer of the soul. You must adhere to the spiritual laws that govern you, for these are the greatest forces of all.

"Even though we are mainly discussing cancer, you can name any disease that you like. All diseases will respond favourably to Spiritual Healing. For example, if your motor car does not start, where does the fault lie? Is there petrol in the tank? Is there something wrong with the engine or the tyres? Are you going to waste time trying to get the engine to start if you have not got petrol in the tank? What is the engine of your body? It is the mind. What is the petrol of your body? It is the bloodstream. What corresponds with the tyres? It is the lymphatic system. This is the system that enables the intelligence to be governed or directed to where it is vitally needed.

"For example, let us consider cancer of the skin. Cancer of the skin is usually either caused by chemicals entering into the skin, usually at your place of employment, which can become poisonous. Equally, if you lie in the sun for hours, this too will cause skin cancer by the drying up of the tissues of the sebaceous glands. These are the glands that supply fluids to your skin to maintain it in a supple condition. How would you deal with such skin cancer? As I have previously said, you would first attack the problem through the mind. Work on the mind. What has caused the

164

condition in the first place? If it has been caused by your place of employment, then you should first obtain protective clothing to prevent exposure to those chemical substances which are poisonous to the body, thereby preventing contact with your skin. If the cancer is caused by over exposure to the sun, then cover yourself up. Make sure that you cover yourself well, since today, the sun can penetrate very deeply because of the reduction of the ozone layer. The Healer can still help by directing the healing, which is God's force. If you can catch any disease in time you will be able to overcome that cancerous state, if you approach it in the correct way. Search your mind and that of your patient. Don't just give the patient the 'Laying on of Hands' week after week. Find out what kind of person the patient is. Are they covetous? Are they spiteful? Are they very nasty-tempered? Do they always want their own way? Are they never willing for anyone else to have their say? Find out!

"As you observe and obtain such information, then you will get onto the right track that will lead you to a successful cure. The more you ask of us in the Spirit World, the more we like it. The more we like it, the more knowledge we can pour into your minds. The thoughts that we pick up are able to get to the root-causes. These causes may have been lying dormant for many many years. As much as fifteen or twenty years, or even more. As the disharmony becomes more firmly fixed, so the body loses its grip on good health. You become ill and go to visit the hospitals, where chemotherapy or radiotherapy may be necessary. When this is finished, the doctor may prescribe another treatment or even another. In this interim period, the doctors themselves will query and question through their intelligent minds. 'Why can't we get positive results?' they may ask. Even though they may have numerous laboratory tests, they still cannot find the cause of cancer. This is because they are working purely and simply on the physical level rather than working on the mind. If they were able to carry out more psychiatric work, they would be on much firmer ground.

"Until recently the doctors have been reluctant to work and blend with Spiritual Healers. In the past you had Spiritual Healing Channels who were working as 'Lone Rangers'. Later they decided that they would like to work with others so that collectively they could attend seminars, conferences, so as to learn the answers to the many diverse problems. From there they were able to return to their own Healing Sanctuaries or churches. They will be able to remember certain events from these conferences and will therefore remember to ask specific questions. This will enable them to enter a higher dimension in the intelligence field.

"They will become more knowledgeable. But why? My medium (Rev. Butler) has been receiving this knowledge for many years. But she always asks why. Why does this disease not respond? By asking such questions and thinking in this way, you will begin to find out. The God-given energy of thought is able to interpenetrate your mind. It will place images there. Sometimes these images are so powerful that the Healing Channel is able to see right through to the direct cause of the disease. Eventually the Healer will be able to unravel all that is injurious or poisonous to the body. You will never know everything, but you will always learn something. Even after you come into my world you will continue to learn. Learn how to blend in with the light, how to blend in with colour and how to blend in with harmonious thoughts. How to blend in with the recorded sounds of music, how to get closer to the animal kingdom. You can heal animals quicker than you can heal children, and children heal quicker than adults. Why? Because an animal knows when it is being loved and cared for and will respond to the pure love of the God-given energy. A child will heal not so quickly because the child may have inherited certain conditions from its mother which may have caused some blockage in the child's mind. Adults are more difficult to heal again! They have problems such as they may have to face insecurity in life. Some may be homeless and may even have to live in cardboard boxes. Adults are affected by all sorts of problems. You must realise that knowledge always continues and is never never wasted.

"For example, look at the government that is in being at this time, in your own country (U.K.). Take for example, Mrs. Thatcher. She discovered that in order to utilise the wealth of the country it was necessary to cut expenditure on certain items. She found it necessary to cut back on the National Health Service by introducing privatisation. What was the effect of this? In my opinion, she was being powerfully used by my world of Spirit. In privatising the hospitals, the poor and the humble were unable to attend hospital, and the waiting lists grew longer. But they were able to attend Healing sanctuaries and churches where Spiritual Healing is given. This two-tier medical system that you have today was produced by thought. Consequently those who are wealthy received the second best treatment. But the poor, the meek and the humble get the best spiritual treatment and they get better. As a result, this two-tier medical system has effectively boomeranged around upon itself. More knowledge has been given to this country of yours. Although financially you may be relatively poor since the financial resources are also poor. But spiritually you are abundantly rich. Yours is the only country that has made Spiritual Healing legal and many countries would like to be under the umbrella of that thought. Consequently there is an expansion of this thought process which is going out far and beyond your local Sanctuaries and churches. It goes out into the world that is around and about you. Look at the flags that surround you in this church in which you are sitting today. They are increasing in number, this church has not asked people to bring their flags here. People have asked this church to accept their flags. There is another flag coming and then another and another. A request has come from France. A request has also come from Yugoslavia. The purpose of the Yugoslavian flag is to bring peace to that country. Thought has to heal the mind, so as to impregnate the disharmonies that are in those countries.

"There is disharmony in Africa, South America, Brazil, the whole world is undergoing strife. Why? By the year Two Thousand there will be total peace in the world. With peace will be brought enlightenment and with the enlightenment will be brought freedom. Freedom from want, anxiety and despair which will result in healthier nations.

"Cancer is in Yugoslavia today. It is cancer of the mind. The cancer which wants to destroy families. When you talk about cancer, it must be realised that it is indeed a very vast subject. Cancer on all levels, is the destruction of human lives and the destruction of purified cells. Everyone of you in this church today has cancer. Even my medium (Rev. Butler) has cancer. Cancer is the consequence of broken cells that have become disused. Healthy people are able to dispose of these cancerous cells, through perspiration, urination, and the excretory systems, whereas others cannot. Consequently, they get regions of disused tissue which can cause pain and destruction of the physical body. But you can all purify yourselves in order to keep yourselves healthy and alert to the problems of life.

"Earlier I spoke to you about sugar being lethal to the physical body. What we also find as we make our observations, is that people tend to destroy the very essence of which God has created. Also, everyone of you, including my medium, are destroying the basic purified substance that God has made, by being too proud! Some are full of vanity. In which way do I mean this? Everyone has conditions of ebb and flow in the body. For example, in the summertime when the weather is warm, you perspire freely, in the wintertime the pores of the skin close and you

167

urinate more. Consequently you urinate less in the summer than you do in the winter and you perspire more in the summer than you do in the winter. This prevents your body becoming exposed to the cold, frosty conditions of winter which would cause shock to the dermas nerves of the skin. But this is what you good people tend to do: You get up in the morning and you go to the bathroom and bathe your bodies and then you apply different types of lotions so that you can smell nice. In doing this, you block up the pores of the skin which God created to be open. So you think you know better than God! If you just leave the perspiration to come out of your body in the normal healthy manner, you can simply wash it off. By all means put perfumes on your clothes, but do not put them on your skin. Be intelligent in your thinking! You must adhere to these simple laws for He knows better than you do. After all, He made you in the first place!

"There are so many things that you do not take heed of. For example, I have seen people who are suffering from very bad feet. Feet are very essential, for they not only carry your body around, but they can absorb shock, tension, frustration and anxiety. For example, you may be walking down the street and you come across a person to whom you have not spoken for a very long time. You may feel yourself becoming tensed up. This tension can be registered in the feet. Your feet should be able to relieve or cure themselves from this condition, but often they cannot. This may be prevented by the various powders that you put on your feet to keep them dry and fresh. These powders can create bacteria in the body which should not be there in the first place. So it's often necessary for you to sit and think about these aspects. You may wish to meditate, and meditation is a wonderful thing to do. In your moments of meditation, aim to purify your mind and then your physical body. You can then follow the mind and the soul.

"There is nothing to be afraid of in death. Death is merely a stepping-stone from here to there. What most people are afraid of, if they are honest with themselves, is the pain and suffering that they may incur before death. Death itself is painless. If you are afraid to die, it can have a very destructive effect on the mind and the physical body. If you experience such fear, think of the light and think of the beauty that is beyond. Have nothing to fear. Your Spirit does not feel pain. It is therefore very important that the Healers encourage their patients to think along these lines and how they can best fit into life. They can learn to accept the Healing Energy which is extremely intelligent. God is Light and God is Love. Loveth all things that He has created in this wonderful universe. These are the simple and essential things to combat cancer. Look at it from this angle please. If you see a person whose mind is very powerful and strong, that mind can become so strong that it can become a Mogul. What is a Mogul? It is an intelligent mind that can open up avenues which can provide work through creative abilities.

"In my world, what you need is knowledge. What you want in your world is money, money that can buy the things that you want. It is knowledge that buys the things in my world. The Moguls of your world can become very powerful workers, for they study and ponder and work towards providing work for others, by creating factories, etc. Very often you get people who become envious of the Mogul. Are they envious of his or her drive? Don't they realise that the Mogul very often has to take great risks in order to create? They are only envious of the fact that the Mogul has more money than them. How stupid can man be? If you have a job with regular wages and you are in good health and have a loving family, what more do you crave for? What more do you want? I thank God that my medium is one of the happiest people in the world. She always radiates happiness. She always lives according to her means. She is strong in the mind. She is fearless and is prepared to take on a battalion of people. If she is doing that which is right and true, she will see to it that her point of view is heard. You could not change her. But there are others who would envy her but are not prepared to lift a finger to fight for that which is right and true. You have to become a Christian Warrior! You have to become a Spiritual Warrior, a 'go-getter' in order that things get done.

"Where would you be today without my world? Where would anybody be without God? Think also of all the squalor and the disharmony that there is in the world. Look at Northern Ireland today. Look at the Third World, where all those poor children are emaciated through starvation. Their little eyes look so pitiful for they do not have enough sustenance to feed their physical bodies. What is needed, is for a few good Mediums to go there and bring irrigation to the land. But there again, they would encounter black magic that would want to kill them, so preventing the masses from getting that which is needed. The time is coming when all men and women shall be free in this universe which God has created. The end of the world will not come until the 'Lion has lain down with the Lamb'. Always remember to think rightly, to react rightly, and to move forward. Then you will receive your true rewards.

169

"Each and every one of you are special to God, for it is He who created you. It does not please Him when He sees you falling down and straying from the right pathway of life. Be in good cheer, for there is always a helping hand, and God is always there to help you. This ends my lecture to you about cancer and I am now open to you to answer any questions that you may have."

There followed a series of questions from the audience sitting in the church. The first questioner asked if the different forms of cancer were associated with different attitudes or personalities.

Dr. Clive Osborne answered as follows:

"Yes. For example, if you are of a jealous nature, the cancer will attack the spleen, where the leucocytes will multiply, which in turn will destroy the physical body. Alternatively, if you are very worried and become hurt, this will cause an imbalance in the thyroid glands, which in turn will cause a lack of thyroxin in the blood. Thyroxin is one of the basic raw materials for the formation of bone marrow. If you have cancer of the stomach, it can be triggered off at two levels. You may be the type of person who is full of worry and tension and you may be over-indulgent in sugar. Your liver may not be able to tolerate it. Cancer can also be produced from the over-production of enzymes in the gastric juices which are necessary for the proper digestion of food. Worry can cause an over-production of the gastric juices. In such cases, you must channel your thoughts towards the parasympathetic nerve-endings to restore the balance, i.e. you must put the 'brakes' on the system. Alternatively, if you were not producing sufficient gastric juices, you would channel your thoughts to the sympathetic nerve-ends, so as to accelerate the production of juices.

"Remember, if you are treating the thyroid glands, don't forget to treat the adrenal glands as well. The adrenals, which are situated above the kidneys, maintain the blood heat within the body, so that your body is maintained warm and in a strong, healthy condition."

The second questioner asked: "At the moment I am undergoing difficulties myself and in the next week I have to go as an outpatient and see a psychiatrist in a psychiatric hospital. Is this Spirit's way of answering my prayers by treating me this way?"

Dr. Osborne replied: "Yes, we work in conjunction with the Earth Doctors. We also work to find out what is upsetting your mind. I have never seen you before, but may I say this to you: If you go back to the period when you were seven or eight years old, you had a very traumatic experience then. You either hit a tree or a tree fell on top of you. Is that correct?"

The second questioner replied: "I cannot go that far back in my mind. But I did undergo a lot of trauma in my childhood."

"Would this be when you were in your sixth or seventh year?" enquired Dr. Osborne.

"Yes. It was around about the seventh year," replied the questioner.

I also feel that you have caused an imbalance. I am also registering a pain here around your liver area. Do you have to hold your side?" asked Dr. Osborne.

"Yes," replied the questioner.

"Are you also aspiring to be a Healer?" asked Dr. Osborne.

"Yes."

"It should be possible for you to help to heal yourself. Ask the Healers who are working with you to go back to that period of time when you were about seven years of age, when you underwent that trauma. They should aim to dislodge it and aim for good influences to come into your life. You can also place your own hands on your liver area and aim to dislodge the shock from the body. Were you involved with lightning or a thunderbolt?"

"I can't remember at this moment in time," replied the questioner.

"But light does affect you?" asked Dr. Osborne.

"Yes," replied the questioner.

"I felt that a thunderbolt came towards you which hit a tree, which in turn hit you. It did not do serious damage to you, but it did register some pain. You must aim to dislodge the pain and the shock through the healing power of God. Also work upon your Earth Psychiatrists for they will also be able to help you."

The third questioner explained that she had undergone the trauma of divorce and asked how this could be affecting her.

Dr. Osborne replied as follows:

"It is a bit difficult for me to talk to you and advise you without discussing your problems here in public. You can send your thoughts out to me, for I can read your mind. But let me begin by saying that you tended to attach a lot, if not nearly all the blame onto your husband. You must also admit that there was also some blame on your side. You did something to upset him and this reverberated by him reacting against you. In order for you to get better and get the best for yourself, you must learn to forgive your husband. In forgiving him, you too will be forgiven for what you did. Then turn your love towards your thyroid, parathyroid, pancreas and your digestive system as a whole. Although you are receiving healing here, do your own healing also by cleaning your own body through your mind. Start asking yourself these sorts of questions: 'Perhaps I did not do this or that in the correct way?' As you forgive him you will receive ample benefit yourself. Remember that you must also ask for forgiveness for yourself. You must do it completely. Only then will good health return to your body."

Another lady asked a question about her daughter who had been suffering from a virus infection and was now affected by rheumatoid arthritis. How could she be helped?

Dr. Osborne said this:

"You must heal the mind, the soul, as well as the physical body. For example, my medium (Rev. Marian Butler) picked up a nasty virus which resulted in a highly inflamed throat, which in turn attacked her chest and joints. She felt 'fluish'. That was only a week ago. Today she is vastly improved and I am using her body to speak to you. Why was it that she was able to make such a quick recovery? It was because she took herself in hand. She is not a perfect person. If she was, she would not be wanted on the Earth Plane. She took herself in hand by working on her own thoughts and her own actions as she goes through life. You can't have disharmony in the body, if you think harmoniously. There has to be harmony in the environment. Thoughts have a very potent effect on the physical body.

"The rheumatoid arthritis which is affecting your daughter will become much better. During the time she had her accident, there was also a lot of stress in the mind. Is that not true?"

"Yes," replied the mother.

"There is also a lot of stress and worry in her life. She is not fitting into life is she?" asked Dr. Osborne.

"Yes," the mother once again replied.

"We all suffer from this at times. It is this shock and the trauma that has caused the rheumatoid arthritis. However, the disharmonised thoughts were there before this, which in turn gave ample time for the disease to take hold of her body. Now reverse this order. Remember to try to cast off your worries. Let God steer you. Ask God to use you so that you can steer your vehicle through life. Don't get into that driving-seat yourself. People are wanting to do too many things at one time in their minds. They undergo one trauma after another, they have not eliminated any of them, before wanting to do something else, etc., they overbalance themselves. You must aim to clear the mind and let God direct you to where you are needed. You have to go the right way, so let Him steer you."

The next questioner asked: "Will the doctors in our world ever become fully aware of the side-effects of the tablets that they issue, and will their attitudes change?"

Dr. Osborne replied:

"Yes. Their attitudes are changing now, because the doctors are allowing Spiritual Healers into the hospitals. Only this week a doctor made arrangements for my medium to attend the local hospital to treat a patient. This shows that there is harmony of thought taking place between the medical and non-medical fraternities. We must all work together. My medium is used by us doctors in the Spirit World, likewise, my medium and I work with the Earth Doctors. We should all work together, including the doctors, surgeons, and psychiatrists, because we all have something to contribute to life. As time progresses, you will all merge together and learn together. For example, Jasmine here (i.e. the Rev. Gwenda Jones) is currently the Vice President of the World Federation of Healing. She is going to encounter some very interesting experiences. With these experiences, together with the discussions that will take place, she will see the outpouring of energy that will take place. They will begin to evaluate her work, which in turn will result in the merging together of thought.

"In Scripture, Saint Paul, who was the Apostle of the Gentiles (i.e. the non-Jewish races), and Saint Luke, were close friends and worked together. Saint Luke was a medical doctor and he worked with Paul. In fact he could work better with Paul than he could with Peter. Paul was a learned man, and found that he could blend with Luke and was in harmony with him. So you can see this process started many centuries ago. Many, many years later they used to burn mediums at the stake and call them witches, since they did not want this enlightenment to be given to the people. Those who carried out such acts will have to pay the penalty for their wrong-doings when they come into my world. For what you sow, you reap.

"Today, it necessitates that you will return to those Biblical times when you will blend and work together. Doctors are also learning that diseases cannot be overcome simply by drugs alone, be they administered in tablet form or in the form of chemotherapy or radiotherapy. They will also find that the greatest radiation which can be given to the body is the energy of pure love, which is the most powerful radiative force in the whole universe. When that day comes, there will be a complete blending of thought."

After Dr. Osborne had finished answering the questions, he paused for a few moments and then continued, pointing his finger to one of the ladies in the audience.

"I want to come to you, the lady whose mother is ninety-odd years old. I hope you don't mind me saying this, but she is travelling very, very quickly into my world for there have been some dramatic changes in her little body in the last four days of your earth time. We know about her, and with your own Guides, we will attend to her. We also have a gentleman here (i.e. in the Spirit World) whose name is Mr. Badry. He sends his love to you and says that he is also helping her. I would like to thank you for your devotion to her and the loving care that you have given her. What you have sown, you will reap in abundance. God Bless you."

Another questioner asked Dr. Osborne what his thoughts were on A.I.D.S.

Dr. Osborne said the following:

"A.I.D.S. is the consequence of the breaking of natural law. It can also affect innocent people and can be passed on to them by infected blood or hypodermic needles. I am also appalled at some of the wards in the hospitals which have become very dirty, which have effectively become germ breeders. One day they will have to revert back to the use of matrons, who will once again bring back law, order, and discipline to the hospitals. I know this does not answer the question you put to me about A.I.D.S. Many, many innocent people can suffer from A.I.D.S. Little children can be born with A.I.D.S., contracted from their parents. You will find that you will have to revert back to more purified thought processes.

A.I.D.S. is not a new disease, it even existed during the times of the Romans. The great Roman emperors used to practise intercourse with their sisters and even dead bodies. These people were rotten to the core. Through such permissiveness, different germs would mix, and it is not normal that they should mix in such a way. Such bodily fluids are not complementary to each other. The consequence of the mixing of such cells, in turn creates disease. One day you will find a cure for A.I.D.S., but people will have to alter their attitudes and thinking before it will be completely eradicated. A.I.D.S. will not be cured by material means, it will be cured by spiritual means and through right thinking."

In closing, Dr. Osborne said: "It has been a pleasure talking to you all today, and I am sure it will not be the last time. There were many people who could not come here today who were cancer victims and wanted to ask questions about their own bodies, but the weather prevented them from coming. My medium had many phone calls this morning, asking for another talk. This will take place later on. I say to those of you who wish to aspire to be good Healers to carry on and offer yourself to God, because He can use you. To others, work on your own self-healing of your body and work with the healers, as you lend yourself to that purified state with God. My love be with you, and my assistance I give to you. My peace be with you at this time and always. God bless you, and good-bye to you."

SO COMES THE CLOSING OF A DAY,
'TIS TIME TO THINK, TO PONDER
UPON THE PAST'S DREAMLIKE WAY,
'TIS TIME TO REST AND WONDER.
COME FLY WITH ME PAST MINDLESS DOUBTS
UNTO REALMS OF UNKNOWN GRACE,
THROUGH AVENUES OF POLISHED PEARLS,
TRIMMED WITH PURE, WHITE LACE.
COME SEE THE ROCK UPON THE SAND,
UPON THAT OTHER SHORE
THAT STANDS SO FIRM, SO SURE AND GRAND,
THE KEY TO GOD'S OWN DOOR.
HUSH, 'TIS SILENT BUT FOR THE FLOW,
BUT FOR THE EBB OF EACH WAVE,
WITHIN THAT POWERFUL RUSH IT ENDOWS,
BEYOND THE EARTHLY GRAVE.
A VOICE IS CALLING FROM AFAR
THAT CALLS OUR EVERY TEST,
A VOICE THAT'S HEARD FROM STAR TO STAR

BY THOSE WHOSE LIFE IS BLESSED.
HE CALLS OUT IN THE DARKNESS,
HE CALLS OUT IN THE LIGHT,
"COME SAVE MY WORLD FROM BLEAKNESS,
COME SHOW MY WORLD MY SIGHT."
SO HERE WE HAVE A LADY
WHO HEARD HER MASTER'S CALL,
WHO ANSWERED THROUGH HER DUTY,
AND THROUGH HER WORK FOR ALL.
WE LOVE YOU, DEAR MARIAN,
JUST FOR BEING YOU,
WE SEE THAT LIGHT THAT SHINES SO BRIGHT
IN EVERYTHING YOU DO.
THE CROSS THAT YOU HAVE CARRIED
THROUGHOUT YOUR NOBLE LIFE,
IN SACRIFICE TO MANY,
THAT HEALED THEIR PAIN AND STRIFE.
THE WORDS THAT YOU HAVE UTTERED
IN TRUTH FOR THOSE TO HEAR,
THE WORDS OF THAT HOLY BIBLE
THAT CASTS AWAY ALL FEAR.
THE TIME YOU SPENT SO LATE AT NIGHT
AS THAT CLOCK TICKED HOURS AWAY
YOU ANSWERED THE LETTERS OF TROUBLESOME WOES,
YET ALWAYS FOUND TIME TO PRAY.
YOU'VE TRAVELLED OVER OCEANS
FROM SHORE TO SHORE TO SHORE,
YOU'VE CAPTURED MANY INSIGHTS,
YOU'VE OPENED MANY A DOOR.
AND SO THIS TROPHY STANDS TO SAY,
ALTHOUGH THE WORLD IS WIDE,
IT NEEDS MORE MESSENGERS LIKE YOU
TO HELP, TO SERVE, AND TO GUIDE.

A prayer of thanks.

Chapter Twelve

LIFE IN SPIRIT

In April, 1992, Raheede, my very dear Friend and Door-keeper, addressed an audience at the Temple of Light Church, whilst I was in the trance state. The subject about which he chose to speak through me was 'Life in Spirit'. I have on many occasions been asked what life is like in Spirit after physical death occurs. Who better could explain this than a soul who is already in the Spirit World himself. The following is a verbatim transcript of what Raheede had to say about 'Life in Spirit'.

"As you begin to leave physical life your Guides or Mentors come close to you, to escort you to your new abode. If you have laid on the bed of sickness, the first place they will take you to is to the 'Halls of Healing'. Remember, I will address you many times this afternoon and I will relate to you the teachings of the beloved Nazarene who you call Christ. When he was on the Earth Plane he stated that:

'In my Father's House are many mansions and were it not so I would have told you. I go to prepare a place for you and where ye shall be I shall be also.'

"Let us return to the physical body that has just made its advent into my world, which may be full of sickness in the mind. Remember that the body is no longer there. It does not exist in my world. There is no pain in the body, but a reactionary pain is retained in the mind. That is why it is necessary for the soul to be escorted into the 'Halls of Healing', so that your minds can be re-educated to realise that you have a brand new body. A body that will remain with you to eternity. A body that is full of wonderment about what it has discovered. A highly intelligent body. As you realise that you have surmounted death, the first place that you make for is home, for you want to share with your loved ones that death does not exist anymore. It is a wonderful place, far better than the Earth Plane. We can do anything that we like through the thought processes.

"In my sphere of life I find that time has no meaning. We do not sleep. We do not sleep for we are continually revolving around the creation of life. The Great White Spirit, who not only put the very life into the universe, also put the breath into your body, is still operating. In my world we create and contribute to that great reservoir of energy. We are still also able to feel the love that is created, both on the Earth Plane and in my sphere of life.

Everyone, when on the Earth Plane, has received the opportunity of becoming in attunement with my world. But alas, this is not always so. The gifts of the Spirit that have been endowed on physical channels (mediums) who have often undergone torturous conditions, through man's inhumanity to man, on the Earth Plane. The greatest light that ever entered this universe was the Nazarene, and they crucified Him because of the envy in their hearts, for He had discovered a new awareness that He wanted to share with mankind. The Christ as you know Him, was a clairvoyant, a clairaudient. He was a 'Physical Medium' and a healer of the first order. He was able to produce materialisation and the phenomenon of Direct Voice Communication with the Spirit World. Yet when He left the earth He stated:

'Marvel not at the things that I have done, greater things than this ye shall do.'

Meaning that the generations to come would be able to do greater things, for He had opened the gateway. But in this day and age I am so grateful to the Great White Spirit for enabling me to create this Temple of Light in which you are all sitting today. I am so grateful for having the privilege of serving a human channel. I am proud that despite the bigotry and disorder that went on through the years, my medium and I won through in the end. We shall go on progressing. We shall further man's capacity to think, because they will begin to realise what can be created through the thought process.

"Even to this day the orthodox church is still putting up barriers to the truths of the Spirit World. They read about it and preach about it to their congregations, but do not practise it. My friends, the Great White Spirit cannot be placed in such a closet. You are too small to prevent the things that He can create. More enlightenment will come. Greater things shall be performed. The Earth Planet shall be saved from man's meanness, spitefulness, and bigotry. The nations of the Third World today, are crying out for sustenance and nourishment which is being denied them. It is being denied for many reasons, many of which are beyond your understanding. But the day will dawn when your mediums on earth will be able to bring about nourishment of those people everywhere, irrespective of race, colour, cast or creed. So that all unfortunate people can be nourished and be free to be given the opportunity to do whatever they want to do in your world, and be free to share the prosperity of the Great White Spirit with you and all other good people of earth.

"You have nothing on earth to compare with that which we have in the Spirit World. Your famous composers of earth received their inspirations from the Great White Spirit. Similarly your poets, scientists, and the numerous great theologians of earth have received their wisdom, simply because it has been revealed to them. There is nothing in your world that can compare with the treasures that we have in our world. There are beautiful colours that you have never seen. There are creatures and plants and flowers which are no longer visible to your eyes. They no longer exist in your world because of man's inhumanity to his lesser brethren in the animal kingdom.

"The diseases in your world are becoming well known to us. Your drugs are not the answer. Answers will be found when man fully understands his spiritual powers. Man will have to turn to the basic truths of the teachings of the Nazarene. Jealousy, maliciousness and spitefulness will have to be destroyed. You will create a new world of love and out of this new world of love, there will be no germ, virus, or disease that can stand in its way. I say to you, just as the Nazarene did when he was on the Earth Plane. If the mediums of your world were to be silenced, the very stones of the buildings from which they are made would crumble to dust. But you are moving forward. I know that when I look around me in my world and when I talk to the various councils that we have; the councils of peace, the councils of healing, the councils of learning, and the councils of music, etc. There are councils of many kinds which reverberate around the pulse beat of pure love that the Great White Spirit has created.

"Love creates knowledge that has no width; no breadth, no depth, it is fathomless. You do not know how the bones of a child grow in its mother, in the uterus. You do not know how the deep crevices of the brain affect the different parts of the body. Such knowledge can seep through from the Creator God, to enable you to understand how these things work. Nothing takes place by chance. In our world everything is a planned act, intelligently governed. From the framework of these laws, many things can be done. I want to prophesy to you about the deceitfulness of man's thinking. The governments of your world are saying that you are almost out of the world of recession. I tell you my friends, the full impact of the recession on earth is yet to come. Man will have to learn that he has yet to stop and retrace his steps. There are those who are searching for more and more, at the expense of those who are starving and who do not have any say in the matter. Such things will have to change.

"I want you to come with me on a little journey of thought. Let us enter into a homestead where there is someone who has fallen sick. The doctor comes and makes his examination. He will decide that the problem is too difficult to deal with and may transport you to the hospital. There they may have to carry out some sort of test before they are able to decide what type of treatment or drug to give you. But there is no drug that will treat jealousy or the selfishness of mankind! It is only the ingredient of pure love that can do this. So you will enter into this thought process.

"The government in your country (U.K.) has effectively decided to have a two-tier system in the Health Service. Those who have money will have the best treatment and those who have no money have to get in the queue and may receive no treatment at all. For it is said there is not enough money to treat all the demands and there is nothing that can be done about it. Yet you must be intelligent in your thinking. The patient will turn inwardly, either in prayer, in pain, or in fear; fear of death, although it does not exist, or fear of the unknown. Will you know anyone when you die? Will you be in a state of emptiness or loneliness? Is there another world? Will you have to suffer the physical torment of the body for evermore? At the other end the Great White Spirit who has created life under the directions of pure love listens to your voice. He will say: 'Wait my child, there is help on the way.' No matter what disease you have suffered from, it can be helped and mastered by reaching out to the higher realms of your inner being. You will receive the dynamic strength that can enter through the mind into the physical body.

"God, your God, my Great White Spirit, is never to be made a fool of, He is never cheated. Nobody can cheat the Great White Spirit; truth will prevail. Truth has to be administered and revealed to the masses at large, so that they can understand how the rhythmic pattern of the Spirit works.

"I refer to one of your past Prime Ministers, Mrs. Thatcher. I am not here to condemn her or anyone. I am here to expand your consciousness and thinking, so that you can see how things are dealt with in my world. Mrs. Thatcher and her government naturally felt that the National Health Bill was too heavy for the country to bear, resulting that almost everyone would have to pay for their treatments. Unknown to her, she had become an instrument of the Great White Spirit. In your country (U.K.) she has set the pattern of dividing the Health Service effectively into two camps. But she has given you a great gift, you ought to get down on to your knees and thank her! Because those people that cannot afford to pay will go to the Church and the Healing Sanctuaries for help, which will result in them receiving the very best treatment for their diseases. Those who you consider to be rich people will afford to go to the doctor and the hospitals or private nursing homes, but will receive second-best treatment. The best therapy is that which comes through from the Spirit World. Man has been given the choice of which methodology to follow.

"When a patient turns to the Spiritual Healer, what happens? You must realise that before a healing can be accomplished, a change has to take place in the mind and soul. The wholeness of man will also have to change before you can have a healthy world. This means that man will have to have a deep appreciation of the Great White Spirit and his wonderful Healing Ministers in my world. If man could only set aside the general bigotry that is in the mind and instead channel his thoughts to that which lies in the World Beyond! What a revelation that would bring. The doctors, the physicists, the scientists, all those learned people are in their laboratories through thoughts that have been created by the mind. They are trying to find out where the true cause of the diseases lie. You know that before a healing can take place the cause first has to be removed. This is where the Spiritual knowledge of my world will play its part and help you to be furnished with the truth. Such truth is not withheld from anyone and it can be revealed to all. Yet not all will want to become Spiritual Healers. Some will think that the Spirit World, my world, is still nonsense. But in time they will be able to compare and see what can be accomplished by the Spiritual Healers.

The Healers will bring about the healings through pure love and intercessionary prayer. In turn, conventional or traditional medicine will effectively want to jump on the bandwagon and try to do what the Spiritual Healers will do, and yet they will still want all the money. Those who think that way will not receive the healing power, it will not be given to them. Such healing power has to be earned through desire and knowledge. I am very proud to inform you that it is not chance that has brought you good people together this day. It is a planned act which has been brought about by greater forces than I. I am only a mouthpiece or a spokesperson for my world, who speaks through my Medium. There are far greater forces on the other side of life that control and steer the ship to a safe harbour. This church (Temple of Light) in which you are sitting today, is a beautiful church and we are so proud of what is being done here. It will, however, be inadequate and will have to expand in order to answer the calls that are coming. They will come from the north, the east, the south and the west, from all over the world. All men will realise, that no matter what nationality, they still have to obey the natural law of the Great White Spirit. Although you are all the same and equal, you do not all react or think in the same way. All souls will have to realise that there is but one Supreme Being and He only should man serve.

"I am so happy today to tell those of you who are Spiritual Healers or are training to be so, that you will in the near future be given greater power. For in the laboratories in my world they have completed their work in finding a cure to cancer. We are also investigating A.I.D.S. Both cancer and A.I.D.S. are not new diseases. Cancer has been around for a long, long time, longer than I can remember. In my world, I cannot measure time, for I exist in a timeless zone. You people live in a time world. I only live in the now, in the present. However, we envisage that the outlook for the Earth Planet is encouraging. True, as I have said, you are entering into a financial crash throughout the world. But, from there, there will be a rebirth of thinking. None of you will starve, for you will all learn to share with each other. It will have to be done that way if you are to be assisted. What could you do if it were not for the rain that descends from the heavens? What if the air that you breath was denied you but a small moment of time? You would not be able to live! See how great He is and how in comparison, how small you are.

"I am not here to make you despondent, I am only here to speak to you and to help you to understand the natural laws that govern you. I am happy to tell those of you who are here today that there are some chosen ones, because they share within them, the very substance of which is needed. For example, I come to you my brother (Lyonel Thomas), who is sitting in the back of the church. You were called a long, long time ago and the suffering that you have endured in life, has allowed you to have a richer awareness of the physical body. I know of no Healer that has escaped suffering. You all have to suffer. How can you appreciate the suffering of others without experiencing suffering yourself?

"There is a friend of this church, who does not live far away, who is a great bastion. I refer to Marian Bruland of Denmark. She feels her country is going to victimise her. She feels the power of the Spirit behind her, yet she feels so alone. They will hound her via the press and television. They will hound her on the streets where she walks. She will surmount these problems, because the soul who is guiding her will see to it that there is a greater awareness brought to bear in that country, so that the whole of the Scandinavian countries may be healed of their cancer cases by the medicine that has been given to her to share with mankind. She will also be instrumental in helping the A.I.D.S. sufferers. But she will first have to suffer some more before the reality of her work is fully realised by the people. I ask you to share this information with her.

"I also feel, my brother, that you have been chosen to bring light into the orthodox church and to break down the position of ill-belief and prejudice. They preach about the healings of the Nazarene and his teachings, yet they are not prepared to fully accept that part of his teachings which can help to heal the nations. Is it not true that amongst those who you work with, you are already finding bigotry? ("Yes," replied a member of the audience.) You will find it more and more until man realises the purpose of the Scriptures. They go to the theological colleges to learn about Scriptures. But they are never taught how to practise the Scriptures or how to produce the vast reservoir of energy that can heal and feed the people.

"Let us go back to the time of the sacrifice of the Nazarene, when he surrendered His Spirit to the Great White Spirit, his Heavenly Father. The veil of the orthodox temple in Jerusalem was rent in two. That was to denote that man must not do things behind a curtain that cannot be revealed in front of that curtain. Knowledge must always be shared and given freely. Do you know that even this day, that in the orthodox churches, they are saying that the Nazarene is at the side of the Great White Spirit and that he is there sitting on a throne? It is utter fallacy! False information! The Nazarene is in the lower Astral Planes, becoming a saviour of souls, trying to uplift man from the degenerate state which he is in. He expresses His love to all because He does not like what He sees in the crevices of the earth, in the darkness of the minds of despair. Even at this late stage, He lends a hand to receive them. It says in the

Scriptures: 'Hitherto where my father works I work also.'

"His world, my world, is an activated-thought world which is able to penetrate into these services and penetrate all states and all dimensions. It can go where it will. Wherever there is life, there is the Great White Spirit.

"No one has ever seen the Great White Spirit, or God, as you call Him, not even in my world. In thought he created you, and in that thought is the Great White Spirit. It is the spirit that moves and breathes in you. His Spirit can be realised in ectoplasmic substances that are formed from the protoplasmic substances of the human body. The protoplasmic substance is the saliva in the body, that beautiful sinovial fluid that keeps the body lubricated. When that protoplasmic substance is removed from the body it can be formed into ectoplasm, which in turn can form materialisations, apports, Direct Voice Communication, levitations, or impart movement. If you were to take the trumpet into the orthodox church today, you would be considered one of the greatest heretics on the Earth Plane. Yet they should read the Book of Revelations, where John the Divine, as he was called, said when he was on the Isle of Pathos: 'There as through a trumpet I heard the voice of the Great White Spirit saying, "I am Alpha and Omega, the Beginning and the End." ' But still they do not believe.

"But those of you who are privileged to work and endeavour to delve into the spiritual fibres of your minds, you are able to perceive these things. You are also able to bring about the reality of thought and be certain that you are able to share it with everyone.

"As you walk, walk tall. If you call yourself Spiritual Healers you become ambassadors for my world. Ambassadors of peace and of love. You must have no envy and always be ready to give and not count the cost. You must love those who despise you. These are the teachings of the Nazarene. It is very difficult to do these things. But if you can do these things, then you are climbing the highest mountain on the Earth Plane. What is it to gain the whole world yet to lose your soul? Yet the more you put into life, the more you can draw out of it. If you find someone who is down, don't just say you are sorry, you must do something about it. Give a helping hand, so as to lift that person out of the mire which he is in. Then you too shall have a reward. For what a man shall sow, he shall also reap. These are the rules and regulations that are laid down. They apply equally in your world as in mine. The more you are able to do, the greater will be your achievements.

"Shortly, I will be releasing myself from your Medium, so that you can have a break, and shortly afterwards I will return through the mental state to answer any questions that you may have.

"I want you to think seriously about my world, for it is not a world to be afraid of. There is nothing for you to fear, for there is nothing but beauty here. But if you have done wrong, then you have cause to contemplate on that which you are in fear of. Even if you have done wrong, do not be afraid. You will always be given an opportunity to correct it and adjust your thinking in the right way. When harmony has been restored, it will enable you to progress even higher along the pathway. I hope that I have been able to tell you this afternoon has been useful to you. My peace I leave with you now. Good-bye to you."

Chapter Thirteen

RECOGNITION

Both Harry Edwards and Dennis Fare felt that the National Federation of Spiritual Healing should become an international organisation. At that time Harry Edwards was thinking of a name that would not omit the term 'Spiritual Healing' from its title. When we held a National Federation of Spiritual Healers (N.F.S.H.) meeting in Hampstead, in 1976, there were many who were against the idea. In addition, we all found it difficult to agree on a new name for the proposed organisation. Mr. Brian Lynch, who was Chairman of the N.F.S.H. at the time, advised us to forget about trying to agree on a new name for the organisation, because quite frankly, he could not see us getting the idea off the ground. Most of us felt that the meeting would end in an anti-climax.

The next day, the Rev. Belding Bingham, of Princetown, U.S.A., told me that he had stayed up all night thinking of a new name for the organisation. The next day Gilbert Anderson was appointed Chairman for the day, and opened the meeting by asking what should be discussed for the day. Almost immediately the Rev. Belding Bingham stood up and said: " . . . before we start Mr. Chairman, I propose we call the new organisation the World Federation of Healing." So I seconded the resolution. There was no amendment to the proposal and the proposition was carrried unanimously. Most of the delegates felt quite proud of the fact that we had at last formed an organisation of international status.

Some time later Dennis Fare and I, on behalf of the World Federation of Healing, were invited to visit the U.S.A. for six weeks. We covered about eight or nine states. I worked in Massachusetts, Rhode Island, Connecticut, Fairfax, Virginia, Kansas City, Missouri and other places that I cannot recall. We did a tremendous amount of healing work there that included visiting various hospitals. Legally, we could have been imprisoned, for Spiritual Healing was not legally recognised in the U.S.A.

The year previous to our joint visit to the U.S.A. I had been privately invited to Palo Alto. Then following the visit to the U.S.A. I was invited to Germany, Austria, and Switzerland. Of all the countries that I have since visited, none has left such a deep impression on me as Austria, for it was there, as you may remember, that I visited the concentration camps of Mauthausen and Dachau. I shall never forget those experiences,

In 1981, I was asked if I was prepared to be nominated to be the first female Vice-president of the World Federation of Healing. At first, I hesitated in giving an answer, since I had never given much thought to holding such an office. Some polite pressure was brought to bear on me to accept the nomination and after much deliberation I eventually decided that I should let myself be nominated. I thought that I would never be elected anyway! It transpired that there were four nominees for the Vice-presidency.

The election of officers took place in Holland, in 1981. You could not believe the shock that I received when I realised that my nomination was accepted and I became elected to the Vice-presidency. After just overcoming the shock of my election, I almost immediately received a second shock, when I realised that in two years time, the Vice-president would be elected to the office of President. It was also agreed that the next W.F.H. conference would take place in Queensland, Australia. I thought that I was going 'down under' to come 'up on top'.

My election to the Presidency, in Brisbane, in 1983, made me realise that at last my work had become firmly established and respected. After the conference I flew on to Los Angeles, Washington D.C., San Francisco, Massachusetts, and finally back home to Wales. Not long after my arrival home, I was interviewed on both radio and T.V. One interview that gave me particular pleasure was when I spoke on the *News Watch Extra* programme on the local radio station 'Swansea Sound'. I have included a transcript of this interview in the book because it will explain to the reader something about the W.F.H. and what it stands for.

The interview was given the following introduction on the radio:

"As concern for the National Health Service grows, more and more people are taking an interest in alternative medicine. Marian Butler is a

187

Spiritual Healer from Ystradgynlais and has just been made President of the World Federation of Healing; the international organisation for holistic medicine. Miss Butler has been talking about her new job to our reporter Liz Lloyd Griffiths:

L.L.G. Can you tell me something about the World Federation of Healing?

M.B. The World Federation of Healing incorporates eighteen countries at the moment and more members are joining us from other countries who are wanting to apply for membership to our organisation. Presently our membership numbers about three hundred, but as I have just said, more are wishing to join us. The W.F.H. is an organised body which incorporates all therapies, not just Spiritual Healing. I am a Spiritual Healer and have been for thirty-four years. There are other branches of healing who are joining us, who recognise the holistic approach to health. It involves not just treating the physical body like a medical practitioner would do, who does marvellous work, we align ourselves with them and we value the good work that they do. We augment that therapy, for example, with Spiritual Healing. Today, the doctors are coming around to this way of thinking. So under the one umbrella of the W.F.H. we have Doctors, Chiropractors, Psychotherapists, Acupuncturists, Spiritual Healers, Homeopaths, Osteopaths, etc. You name them, and they are joining us.

L.L.G. How many members have you got?

M.B. As I have just said, about three hundred.

L.L.G. So it is quite an accolade when you have been honoured by the W.F.H., that someone from Ystradgynlais has been made the World President?

M.B. Yes, but I never asked for this position, but as it is said . . . 'by the fruits of thy labours ye shall be known.' I never asked to be nominated. But I was first nominated as Vice-president in Holland, in 1981. I was elected two years later in Brisbane, Australia.

L.L.G. So you have been a member for many years?

L.L.B. Yes, originally I was a Charter Member. I was the person who seconded the resolution which gave the organisation its name in the first instance, i.e. the World Federation of Healing.

L.L.G. Has the very fact that you are a Spiritual Healer got anything to do with the fact that you are President? Are Spiritual Healers recognised as being the top?

M.B.   No. We share the Presidency. Following myself will be Dr. Carol Brierly from Huddersfield who is an Allergist and Dermatologist. She is currently Vice-president of the W.F.H. and she will follow after me when I finish in two years time.

My election to the Presidency of the W.F.H. expressed some of the finer aspects in my life. The many tribulations, humiliations and rejections over the years were at last over and my work had become recognised in many parts of the world. I have always tried to follow the Christian pathway wherever I have been. I often ask myself if I have reached the zenith of my Spiritual Healing work. I truthfully cannot say, because I truthfully don't know what God has in mind for me to do.

In July, 1985, at the end of my Presidency, I organised our W.F.H. conference at Clyne Hall in Swansea University. Members from eighteen countries were in attendance from as far as Australia, South Africa, Canada, U.S.A., and Greece. Several other members from countries in Europe and throughout the U.K. were also represented. Of the many ethnic groups present were two members of the North American Indian nations, namely Vera Martin and Eileen Fitzner, whose ready charm and friendliness endeared them to all present. A large number of daily visitors from many parts of Wales attended lectures and joined happily in all our proceedings.

During one afternoon I had arranged a bus trip to the Bardic Stones in my home town of Ystradgynlais. There we formed a circle around the stones, said our prayers, and our Welsh contingent closed the service with the singing of *Land of my Fathers*. From Ystradgynlais we continued on our trip to the Black Mountains where we all enjoyed a picnic to the accompaniment of the birdsong and the occasional bleats of grazing sheep. The conference ended on a Friday evening with entertainment by 'John and Jean' with excerpts from the popular shows. This was followed by the Ystradgynlais Male Voice Choir, who gave many songs from their vast repertoire. Then dancing passed away the hours until midnight, so closing a very successful week of Conference and the end of my Presidency, which I handed over to Dr. Carol Brierly.

On the home front, my own work was being recognised more and more and the bastions of prejudice were falling down. This gave me a sense of deep-felt joy and happiness, for at last all that I had worked for and stood for was being recognised by the public at large. This also made me realise that the time was ripe for me to build my own church. A church that would be worthy of God and the work that we were doing for Him.

We had already purchased a strip of land opposite my Sanctuary. I felt compelled to purchase it for the church ever since the miracle that happened there during the Coal Strike of 1926, when I was but a young girl of eleven years of age. As the strike had already been in progress for many months, the poor miners faced a bleak winter without any means of heating their homes. The women were forced to search the local parks and copses for wood to collect and store in preparation for the forthcoming winter. It began one summer's day when the weather was exceptionally hot. Consequently the miners decided to make two swimming-pools in the river adjacent to land on which the church stands today. One pool was smaller and shallower, being just deep enough for the young girls and boys to paddle in, with the second being larger and deeper, providing an adequate depth for the men to swim in.

At that time, I was just a young observer sitting on the bank in a chair, recuperating from one of the many illnesses that I had suffered, when suddenly one of the young boys gave out a loud scream from the centre of the paddling-pool. From my position on the high bank, I had a bird's-eye view of the scene that was unfolding before me. They raced to attend to the screaming lad, and as the men lifted him out of the water, I could see that one of his feet was bleeding quite profusely. They carried him to the bank, examined his wound and decided to take him to the local doctor who lived several hundred metres away. Meanwhile, the remaining men removed all the children from the pool and immediately started taking out stones from the bottom of the pool, so that they could search for the suspected broken bottle which had cut the lad's foot.

However, their search was to be in vain. They had not been in the pool very long when the water erupted like a miniature volcano, spurting a black fountain of coal high into the air. Everyone ran for their lives so that they could avoid injury from the sharp, diamond-like lumps of pure anthracite coal which were falling around them. Fortunately nobody was hurt. When the doctor later examined the lad's cut foot, small pieces of coal were found in the wound.

The coal of course was the answer to the miners' prayers. Everyone rushed away to get shovels, buckets and barrows in which to collect the 'black diamonds' that would sustain them through the winter. It was just like a 'coal manna' from heaven. Father collected three tons of coal, my uncle, Aunt Bess's husband, gathered two tons, and our next-door-neighbour had a further ton. Everyone in the street and adjacent streets had more than enough coal to see them through the winter.

In all villages, good news travels fast, just like the drums of the jungle, and it was not very long before the mine owners, 'The Amalgamated Anthracite Company', got to hear of it too. They instructed the police to stop the people from removing coal from the riverside, since they had the mining rights of all the coal in the area. Not long after, the company's coal hauliers arrived with carts drawn by magnificent shire horses, to gather up the remaining coal. Sometime after their arrival, the coal that lay about the riverside became a solidified mass, making it almost impossible to remove. Simultaneously the fountain of 'black diamonds' ceased to erupt anymore. The only coal that was successfully removed from that site was the remains of that which had previously been collected by the poor miners. As I progressed through life, I understood that what I had witnessed was truly miraculous, being but another example of Spiritual Phenomena.

After many decades of saving all the free will donations that we had received, we finally set the wheels in motion to build a church. In 1986 we engaged the services of an architect, Mr. William Hopkins, to design the church for us. We stressed to him that we wanted a church with three separate Healing rooms, a Meditation room, a room of Silence, together with an office, and a small kitchen for serving tea and coffee.

After we had agreed upon the building design, an application for planning permission was put before the Town and Country Planning Office and after much deliberation, planning permission was eventually granted to us. But before it was granted we had to supply a sample of the building bricks that would be used, to ensure that the building was attractive and blended with its surroundings. During Easter, 1986, we held our first service on the land, so that we could consecrate the ground which was in a field opposite my own home and Sanctuary. We later held our usual Sunday Service in the Sanctuary. When the service ended we went outside again and were welcomed by a wonderful sight, the field was carpeted by the purified colour of white snow! We felt that God himself had added his own blessings to the occasion. On the 29th August, 1986, the first foundations were laid and we entombed dozens of prayers in them. This occasion was truly memorable and the workers remarked that they had not witnessed such a scene before. I am not quite sure, but I think they thought that we were crazy!

In November, 1986, I was invited to give a seminar in Wupppertal, Germany. It was during my stay in the lovely home of Giesla Hauthausen that I first saw some beautiful arched doors. I instantly fell in love with them and I asked if could have my photograph taken in front of the doors so that I could use the picture to have a replica made for my own church on return to the U.K.

As each day passed, we all sensed an aura of a new beginning. Finally, on the 14th April, 1987, the new church was officially opened and dedicated. The dedication was carried out by the Revs. Gladys and Kenneth Custance from Massachusetts, while the Rev. Marian Proctor, also from the U.S.A., together with my niece, Rev. Gwenda Jones, administered the opening ceremony. We were also privileged to have with us our friends Cynthia Fitten Carrington from Washington D.C., Irmgard Christoph from Neckerbischofsheim Germany, Dr. Carol Brierly, Dennis Fare, and Gilbert Anderson, together with the local mayor, Mr. Tom Jones, as well as my dear friends and patients from over the years.

The opening of the church was truly a magnificent day for us all, after almost forty years, the church was finally opened. To me it was not just a church, it was the first Christian Spiritualist Church and Spiritual Healing Sanctuary to be opened in Ystradgynlais. As Raheede had predicted those many, many years before, we named it:

The Temple of Light Church and
Independent Christian Spiritual Healing Sanctuary

No one can assess the joy of seeing the wisdom of Spirit actually coming into being. I felt that the church was a building that no one could take away from us and above all, no one could deny the truth, sincerity, love and compassion upon which it is founded. I will never forget that day.

Have we progressed since that day? Of course, the healing energy that continues to emanate from that church is beyond my understanding. Today, my neighbours can look at the cross when it is illuminated at night. Some have informed me of the strength that it has given them and told me that it has sustained them in their hour of need. The healing energy knows no limits, it truly has no width, no breadth, no depth, it is fathomless. Today, more people are seeking from under the branches of the church, the light that can only come from God. For example, about two years after the church opening, there was a man passing by whose heart was very heavy. I do not know his name. He was at breaking-point. Although he never actually entered the church, he told a friend that he had stood outside on the road in front of the illuminated cross and asked God for help. That kind of healing is continuous, it never stops. The symbol of the illuminated cross recalls to me the words of Scripture which say: 'Let your light shine before men so that they may see your good work and glorify the Father, who is in heaven.'

It is through the thought processes that the light is transmitted from the church to the people. We shall never know who they all are! But does it matter? Names are not important, it is their souls that are of the prime importance to God.

In more recent years I seem to be developing an intuitive diagnosis of disease. I feel it is leading me into a field where intelligent understanding of the true cause of disease is obtained. Today we deal with all forms of disease, including cancer, multiple sclerosis, A.I.D.S., heart conditions, internal disorders, skin complaints, the list is almost endless. It is not just sufficient to know about the disease or how it can be cured. I feel very deeply about how the disease was caused in the first place. Where do we go wrong in life? What causes the disharmony in the physical body? I have never considered Spiritual Healing to be an alternative to medical science, but it is very highly complementary to it indeed. Equally, we must all realise that it is God who created the physical body in the first place. He created all types of souls. He created the doctors, musicians, artists, poets, manual workers of the various colours, casts and creeds. As God is Creator of the mind, body and soul, one must give credence to the fact that when things go wrong, it is He who is the one most likely to repair things, for it is He who created it in the first place. For such reasons and logic, I feel that this is why intuitive diagnosis is passed on to us. I feel so strongly about this, that I feel I could challenge anyone, that I could find out the true cause of any illness or disease. In my own mind, I can honestly and truthfully say that I have never failed yet in finding the true cause of the disease. I have found that almost everyone can be helped. Effecting a total cure, however, is not always possible. In some cases the patient has suffered the effects of the disease for many, many years, sometimes decades before he or she has turned to God for help. I cannot stress the point strongly enough that man is comprised of mind, body and soul. He is a whole being and not just a physical body made up of individual organs. Equally, disease can be generated either through the mind, body, or soul.

Doctors do a tremendous amount of excellent work on the physical body and the nursing profession gives them tremendous loyal support in adverse economic circumstances, through their love and dedicated service to mankind. But it is only God who can treat the mind and the soul. It is also God's angels of mercy on earth, be they doctors, nurses, or the numerous alternative therapists that administer to the needs of the sick person.

In the future we must all learn to reach greater heights together, we must learn to work together for the benefit of the sick and not for personal ego or for the financial rewards of the large drug companies. We must learn not to work in opposition. For example, medical science which treats the physical body must learn to work with the Spiritual Healers, who can also work on the mind and soul level. It must also be realised that many diseases have psychosomatic causes and that before a healing can take place, be it a mental or a physical condition, it is always essential to get to the root-cause of the disharmony.

I like to read Scripture not because it makes me feel better, superior or more intelligent than anyone else, but because I like to delve deeply into its true understanding. What did Jesus mean when he said:

' . . . you cannot heal some people, not until the third or fourth generation.'

How can a Healer heal a person 'not until the third or fourth generation'? In my opinion there has to he a link through the mind of the person who is sick in the present generation, with the lineage of past generations. To me, this clearly shows that the true cause of the disease may stem from the parents, grandparents or even the great grandparents. Where is the physical part of the body that permits connection with lineage – where the disease is hereditary?

Before a child is born it may have been subject to a shock or a very traumatic experience within its mother's womb. Such a condition may even be linked with three or four past generations; through the grandmother or even back to the great grandmother. In order to relieve such a disharmony, it is essential for the Healer to place the hands on the patient's navel, for it is through the umbilical cord that the child was linked to its mother.

Similarly, it is the tangible yet invisible Silver Cord that links the Spiritual body with the physical body. In the book of Ecclesiastes it is written:

'. . . ere the Silver Cord be loosen or the Golden Bowl be broken at the cistern, then shall the body return to the earth and Spirit returneth to its Creator.'

There it explains the true cause of many diseases. There is also a need to pool our Healing resources and knowledge, for no one person or profession can understand the whole being. Most medical doctors can only understand certain specialised areas of the physical body, and truthfully, despite all their wisdom and intelligent efforts, even they, do not understand all. Medical science today also knows how to completely match the tissues of transplanted organs and yet in all cases the body seeks to reject the organ. If medical science could be just as meticulous in matching the personality and the mind and the soul of the patients involved in organ transplantation as they are in matching tissue type, I am sure a true matching could take place. However, we all really know how very difficult such a perfect match would be to achieve.

Surely there has to be an answer to all the various kinds of sickness that exists in our world today! There are infants who are unwanted and unloved even before they enter our physical world. I am certain that they realise this as they progress through life. There are also the little babies who are aborted, their little souls too are subject to shock. God had given them a soul so that they could experience physical life and love. Perhaps when their souls return in another physical body, they will be able to experience what physical life has to offer. As we progress on the ladder of life, I am hopeful that the Healing Channels of the future will aspire to a higher level of understanding, a much higher level than most of us are able to achieve today. One thing I am certain about is that, when my earthly life is ended, I would very much like to unite with my Healers who have worked with me through the years. I hope that I shall have the privilege of being able to help them, guide them, and inform them of the new knowledge that I will have accumulated in my new sphere of existence in the Spirit World. I still hope that I will be able to serve humanity from behind the scenes of the Divine world of perfect love and purity.

Beni.

Dear Miss Butler,

My name is Beni Dreiblatt. You may remember me, I was the good looking Dachshund that came to you for healing last year, when my legs were paralized, and I was unable to walk.

I am very sorry for not having been in touch with you sooner than this. I would like to thank you very much for the healing you gave and the kindness you showed me.

I am sure that you will be very pleased to learn that, as from last Autumn, the feeling has returned to my legs and I am once again on my feet and am leading a normal life, able to walk and run.

It took some time before the feeling came back completely and for my muscles to regain their strength. I occasionaly have a cramp in my left leg, but on the whole I am fit and healthy.

Once again I would like to thank you sincerely for your help. I am in no doubt that the healing you gave me was of tremendous benefit to me.

Lots of love and my very best wishes.

Your friend,

Beni.

X

A letter of thanks from Beni's owner.

The new church – opened on the 14th April, 1987.

Interior of the new church.

The Rev. Marian Butler and her niece, the Rev. Gwenda Jones,
at their joint Ordination on the 23rd September, 1989.

Back row: Left to right: Eirwen Harvey, Wayne Jones, John Bowen, John Thorne, Helen Thorne, Barrie Howell.
Front row: Left to right: Carolyn Jones, Clare Cole, Marian Butler, Gwenda Jones, Doreen Howell, Shirley Howells.

202

205